BREAKING THROUGH CONCRETE

The Gift
of Growing Up
With
Mentally Ill Parents

Marifran Korb

ISBN 978-0-9797462-2-0

Published by
Soulful Solutions, a subsidiary of
Be You Productions, LLC
Cincinnati, Ohio

Email: Marifran@MentallyIllParents.com
Website: http://MentallyIllParents.com

Cover Design by Bonnie Schantz
Cover Photo by Morgine Jurdan

This book is dedicated
to all those who live
with any form of mental illness
and to their family members.

It's hard to fight an enemy
who has outposts in your head.
~ Sally Kempton

10% of proceeds from this book go
to develop, support, and promote
mental health education
and advocacy programs.

To provide privacy, some names
in this book have been changed.

Mission of Breaking Through Concrete: The Gift of Having Mentally Ill Parents

To reveal what is behind the curtain of mental illness in family life.

To describe how life barriers do not have to stop you. To relate how joy is available on the other side of the obstacles.

To demonstrate how love is all around you, including where it is unexpected.

To show that love can heal wounds, even if you have to find love outside your home.

To illustrate how mental illness needs medical attention as much as any other illness.

To explain that being born to mentally ill parents does not determine your mental or emotional state.

BREAKING THROUGH CONCRETE: THE GIFT OF MENTALLY ILL PARENTS *is an example of the courage it takes to transform a dream into manifestation.*
~ Marcia Wieder, CEO / Founder Dream University and Best-selling Author of 14 books

ACKNOWLEDGEMENTS

Forever I am indebted to these friends. Without them this book would never have been published. I am profoundly grateful to my friends Marcia Erdman, Lyn O'Brien, and Jane Bath for their encouraging support that kept me writing.

Deep gratitude goes to my friend, Dan Erdman for his loving direction, evoking my focus and purpose.

Great appreciation goes to coach Sheila Finkelstein for helping me clarify my mission, to Coco Fossland for providing needed structure, and to husband Ed Korb for his pure patience and computer skills.

Thank you to Nancy Broermann, Bonnie Schantz, Karen Wythe and Phebe Beiser for their editing skills.

Great gratitude goes to my daughter Ilona Korb for her support formatting the manuscript, to author Michele Stegman for her feedback, and to my brother Edmond Byrne for technical advice on: "Who do you think you are!"

After this book was finished, it took the support of countless friends over many years to publish it.

CONTENTS

INTRODUCTION

First The Concrete   1
I Prefer The Gifts   5
In The Beginning   8

PART ONE: THE FORMATIVE YEARS

Bad   17
The Orphanage   19
Family Lies   27
Quasimodo   29
The Beloved Doll   35
The Lone Window   37
Crime And Punishment   40
How Ice Cream Can Go Wrong   41
Hidden Nurturance   43
My Homework And A Boy's   45
The Aftermath Of One Psychotic Episode   52
Stew   54
"I'll Get It Right Away"   56
"Who Do You Think You Are!"   59
Family Un-Togetherness   61
Christmas Decorations   63
A Living Pin Cushion   67
Secrets   70
What Is Acceptable?   74
Pleasing Dad   76
Money   79
Sibling Bonding Over A Freezer   81
Sounds   84
Mother's Self-Expression   85
The Vbt (Very Bad Times)   89

Hair   94
Love Thy Neighbor   96
Summer Weekdays   100
When The Sun Broke Through   103
The Calm And Then The Storm   104
Dinner   106
The Essay   108
Giving And Receiving   110
Generosity   113
Growing Pains: Lessons In The School Yard   118
The Dance   120

PART TWO: MOVING INTO TEEN YEARS

Endings And Beginnings   126
Clothes   129
Babysitting   132
Supportive Friends   134
Faith   139
My Best Friend's Mother   141
Morning   143
First Date   146
Visiting The Hospital   151
The Treasured Statue   159
School Return   164
College Plan   167
Telephone   170
Driving   175
Encouragement In A Nun's Garb   179

PART 3: EMERGING INTO ADULTHOOD

Break In; Breakthrough   183
College   185

Car Follow Up   186
Finding Kindness From An Unusual Source   189
Drinking   193
Life Is Tenuous   195
Yellow Pages   197
Church Announcement   204
Judy   207
No Escape   208
After School   211
One Visit   215
Communication   217
Parting Thoughts   222

PART 4. MUSINGS ON THE GIFTS

Self-Awareness and Understanding 239
Independence, Freedom and Self-Reliance 243
Perseverance and Preparation ... 246
Patience, Flexibility and Resilience ... 247
Altruism and Compassion   249
Discovering Love, Gratitude, and Integrity 251
Responsibility 254
Detachment 255
Insights and Perspectives 257

PART 5. SURVEY

Survey 261
Survey Results   263

I like living. I have sometimes been wildly, despairingly, acutely miserable, racked with sorrow, but through it all I still know quite certainly that just to be alive is a grand thing.
~ Agatha Christie

INTRODUCTION

FIRST, THE CONCRETE

My parents were my concrete. The emotional concrete had set in before I knew it. Growing up, it seemed solid and impossible to break through.

This concrete story is about the hard reality - the details of living with a disorganized schizophrenic, bi-polar mother and a depressed, closet alcoholic father. My experiences can give you glimpses into the hidden world of mental illness in a family.

Throughout my life, neither my mother nor my father approved of anything that I accomplished, not my graduations, my accolades, or my choices. Though they desperately wanted me to marry, they did not approve of my husband. At every stage of life, I felt unacceptable. Looking elsewhere, I discovered that appreciation and approval could come from others.

There is an undeniable downside to a difficult upbringing. Psychiatrists tell us that human frailties are accentuated in a stress-filled, suppressed, under-protected childhood.

After experiencing emotional neglect and abuse, a sense of shame can be intensely difficult to release. This type of upbringing most often results in unrelenting emotional baggage such as low self-esteem, frustration, and insecurities. One can think: "If my mother couldn't love me, then who could?" That thought lurked in the background for me.

While my mother threatened my life at times, not all mentally ill parents are a danger to their children. Some parents with mental illness could have adequate medicine or behavior modification techniques to control their symptoms. In such cases, the family can function well. The risks to any child with one or more mentally ill parents are on a case-by-case basis.

In no way do I advocate overlooking the serious damage a child can suffer from living with a disturbed mentally ill parent, or parents. While unaddressed mental illness can be the trigger for bad behavior, the results of that behavior still causes undeniable damage.

There are many highly regarded, accurate studies about children's wounds at the hands of a mentally ill parent. Though there is truth in this view, it is not the only way to look at this, or any other challenge. If only the pain is perceived, the problems are emphasized and nothing else is observed.

Up until now, I have not read anything of the benefit of experiencing such a childhood. After having experienced the difficulties firsthand, I learned that my experiences with mentally ill parents could eventually reveal to me my power. It took me quite awhile to get to that understanding. No matter what my past, I can view it as a burden, or a benefit.

How could there be a benefit? For one, even a severely mentally ill parent has their moments of kindness or clarity. Those soft, tender moments in a typical mother would be taken in stride, appreciated mildly at best. The same kindness received from a dysfunctional parent produces pure bliss. That moment of kindness can affect a child throughout his or her life. My chapter: Giving and Receiving is one such example of a rare benevolence, deeply appreciated.

When demonstrations of love are so rare, it could result in a child giving up and becoming cynical about the world. More often, gratitude is automatically there when a child of a mentally ill parent does receive some symbol of love after long, lean times of nothing. From the hard times, something valuable can emerge; something that takes up residence in your soul. It settles there because you had to labor so hard to chisel through it.

While I am not advocating for severely mentally ill people to parent children, my point is that if you are a product of that environment, there are other ways to view your past. You cannot change what happened. You can only change your view of it.

At some point, I recognized that there is a benefit to taking responsibility for my life. To blame anyone else is to cripple, and limit myself.

As a child, I made immature responses that had me experience the solid concrete barriers. As an adult, I have the ability to find the cracks in the concrete. If I only see the limits of the concrete and do not look for the cracks to break through, then I will continue to constrain my life.

The concrete made me who I am in the present. Being "between a rock and hard place," I found the breaks to push through. It took more than one breakthrough to open the way.

All concrete has its weak point. When I was a young adult I saw others unhappy due to their childhood. I knew instinctively that I wanted to be free, and to take charge. Others were banging their head against the proverbial concrete of their life story. Being able to see the confining and punishing part of resisting the past was one of the cracks in the concrete that I grew through.

Yes, I wondered what was the point of all the pain I went through. I wondered why I never wanted to look at my past. Clinging to denial, I refused to examine what bothered me and what kept me stuck. It took many experiences of loving and being loved to allow me the space to open up.

In disclosing raw details, I am not blaming my parents. They were as much sufferers of their illnesses as their children were of them.

My purpose in sharing the inner workings of a household in daily crisis is to speak my truth. Hopefully, my story will help you find your truth.

I PREFER TO FOCUS ON THE GIFTS!

The flower or weed under concrete has power. How many times have suburbanites tried to kill whatever tries to grow through the driveway or walkway at their home? It seems an endless task since the life force is determined to survive. We all have that tenacity somewhere within us.

The positive gifts include the perspective life affords after coming through tough times. One can feel the relief and liberation, knowing that it is no longer the life you have to live anymore.

Since I've been an adult, people often ask me how I got to be such a carefree, contented person. Since I do not try to be happy, I wondered what is it that people see about me. I believe it is that I am in touch with the joy that we all have naturally. Coming from a difficult background allows me a perspective of the treasure that life is. I appreciate my life, since it was not always easy. Pushing beyond the past struggles, I have confidence that I can handle anything that comes up in life.

Another way to look at the gift is to see the strengths gained from such a life. I can trace many constructive traits right back to my childhood. Rooted in my past, I can identify some qualities that I claim most of the time. Just as seeds grow in the dark, moist earth, they break through the rock-solid concrete at some point. For me, the priceless gift was allowing the pressure cooker of such a background to both tenderize and deepen me. In that childhood, I had to take responsibility for myself in order to find my way. It also made me compassionate to others in pain. My parents taught me that I was worthless. Added to that, I was always the shortest child in my class and the scrawniest child anyone knew. My self-perception was my small physical size indicated small value to the world. I expected to get overlooked. Unable to breathe, I felt lower than an animal. In order to survive my own negative assessment, I had to put aside, or forget who I was.

Focusing on each task at hand, I threw myself into each activity before me. It helped quiet that vicious voice in my head that could and would swallow me up with messages such as: "You are worthless." "You are nothing." "You aren't equal to anyone." "You deserve to suffer."

It was not an option to expect my parents to protect me from walking in the extreme cold wind when it overstressed my breathing. Making life easier was not what my parents were about.

Throughout my life doctors have been amazed at how active and energetic I am with the damaged lungs I have. Perseverance and determination to live came directly out of knowing I had no safety net.

My belief is that we possess potential gifts and qualities from birth. Life gives us opportunities to use them and to develop more. A thorny childhood gives you a great many opportunities to use and expand gifts. Each of us chooses when and how to use them. Throughout life we build on the gifts we started.

For those who have experienced a childhood such as mine, may you take heart in what your past experience has given you. May you see the break though the cement from your life story. This book is meant to remind you to discover your particular emergence through your concrete and into the freedom and satisfaction of full self-expression.

Specific gifts are revealed through the book. Part 4 focuses and elaborates exclusively on the gifts.

IN THE BEGINNING

Call me Marifran. My parents named me Mary Frances. Frances was my mother's name. Being the first girl in an Irish Catholic family, I was named Mary, reminiscent of the Blessed Mother. Two mothers, one was blessed and one demonic. I could identify with neither. The demonic mother dominated my childhood with endless cutting words and actions that wounded me. The Blessed Mother did not speak to me, though I prayed, waited, and listened.

As a banshee screaming and hitting, my troubled mother was diagnosed first as schizophrenic and later as bi-polar, too. A hoarder, she had mood disorders and psychotic episodes. An emotional and sometimes physical torture machine, systematically she invalidated me. Chanting an endless litany of my limitations, she made up many of them. My value was not merely neglected. It was seriously trampled.

No one would question that my mother was unstable. She had been diagnosed and hospitalized numerous times. It was hard for anyone to miss noticing her problems, even on a first meeting.

Medical treatment for mental illness had not evolved sufficiently at that time my mother lived. No doctor, no therapy, and no medicine ever worked well for Mother. Her ninety years of life were over in 2003.

My father's persona was a calm, nice exterior. My parents appeared as polar opposites.

It was not that simple.

It is difficult for me to reveal my father's part in the family drama. The many relatives in his family of origin saw an ideal image of my father. Some people who knew him likely would reject the idea of a dark side. There was, and is, a code of silence.

A quiet, intelligent man, Dad's depression dulled any possible empathy for his children's plight. Fearing confrontation, he allowed his unbalanced wife to rule the household and dictate all his days. At the same time that he allowed his wife to emote constantly, he suppressed emotions in his children. While he had numerous splendid qualities, his blind tolerance of his wife's conduct meant that his children were left vulnerable to verbal, and often, bodily attack.

Flanked by a mother who assaulted my spirit and a father who denied my reality, I felt trapped. There was no refuge.

Since denial was the world I grew up in, my relatives and neighbors saw my father as the tolerant and long suffering partner to my mother's aggressive hysteria and narcissistic ways. Dad's depression symptoms went undiagnosed and his drinking was hidden. He continued his civil engineering career until retirement. His illness remained imperceptible, though not invisible.

Many men in Dad's family had the symptoms of Asperger's Syndrome. At social events, my father had noticeable emotional discomfort.

When I grew up, despite having two brothers, I felt alone. They could talk to each other in their shared room. Many times, for instance when they taunted me for momentarily wanting to take ballerina lessons, I knew I was a misfit. Too short, too thin, too sick, I felt I did not belong there. It seemed I did not belong anywhere.

Being the only girl sandwiched between two boys was not an enviable position in a home where males were prized. At different times as adults, both brothers told me that I was the prime target of our mother's wrath. Yet, just living in that house was hard for them, too.

Instead of competing for attention as most siblings do, we three tried to disappear as much as possible in order to stay out of the line of attack. My brothers had to tread carefully. I was vulnerable even while I was careful.

As a child I felt that I had no choice. Having no way to defend myself from the onslaughts of my mother or the passivity of my father, I wanted to be able to say: "Open Sesame" like Ali Baba. My world did not open up.

Besides parents who could not support me emotionally, my body would not support me physically. My parents realized that I had a problem when I turned blue at a year old, nearly dying from breathing challenges. Their conclusion was that *I was a problem.* Being physically ill was unacceptable, even shameful.

According to my mother, a doctor actually had declared me dead during a respiratory incident when I was a one-year old. It would not be the last time that I escaped the clutches of death. I refused to be counted out. As always in my life, I didn't want to miss anything, even if there wasn't much of a party in which to linger. Knowing that I couldn't breathe and I was half her size, my mother took unfair advantage over me. Every chance she had, she used it.

Years later, I paid a lot of money for a fish tank, filling it with tropical fish. I noticed that any ill fish was always attacked consistently by at least one healthy fish. It reminded me of my mother and me. Immediately, I gave away the fish along with the huge tank.

A girl's mother is her model for what the future holds. My mother showed me two views of my possible future. One was that of an absolute slug, and one was that of a runaway steam engine. Every afternoon the slug could be found snoring on the couch in the midst of disarray. Surely, her excessive sleeping was a symptom of hopelessness of ever ridding herself of her demons.

The runaway steam engine mother took various forms. At times, it was dramatic singing. Not an expression of joy, the singing was forced. So were a lot of things. Other times the steam engine shifted from endless talking to sudden, terrible anger usually followed by a blow to my head. That taught me to keep my distance and carefully be vigilant of Mother's movements. In a moment's notice, I was prepared to run fast no matter how distressed my body. Living with a dangerous mother, I had to study her everyday to determine if I had to sprint, or dodge. Given those choices, I was on edge. That seriously lowered my immune system.

Mother's energy was so erratic that I never felt safe. Learning to be ready for onslaughts at any moment, I did not know how to relax. Literally, I sat on the edge seat. Often, Dad, who was uncomfortable with my discomfort, exhorted me to "relax." Confused at having no reference point, I could not respond to his order. It took many years to understand what it meant to relax. In my late thirties, the realization of relaxing occurred while in a group visualization exercise. Though relaxation was a revelation, it was only the beginning. It still took practice even after I experienced it.

It was not merely the lack of emotional affection that hurt. It was the loss of guidance. There was no north star. Having no idea who to turn to, or what to reach for, I did not know what I wanted outside of escape.

While plotting for years to obtain liberation from my early life, I managed to move nearly 500 miles away for college. Leaving meant independence, despite missing my close friends. Freedom did have its price. Struggle was my theme song. On a deep level, my core belief was that "life was difficult." Certain that I deserved a tough life, I also believed that "I could take it." That combination of beliefs ensured an continual loop of struggle wherever I went.

The concrete in my life started out as my parents. Soon it was my unconscious, endless self-negation that kept me stuck. My conditioning skewed my view of myself and the world. Though loving friends mitigated my view, for most of my life I continued to carry feelings of being unlovable, damaged, and separate. That secondary effect of my childhood was the concrete of my making. It proved to be equally as hard to break through, since my mind repeated my parents' messages like a robot with no off switch.

Yet, my bizarre background, in some ways, prepared

me for life. In the midst of physical and emotional pain, I sought love wherever I could find it as early as I can remember. So many loving people helped me grow. People who did not even know me, contributed to me. Some who did know me loved and appreciated me, too. Each of them nurtured me and provided something that I needed. Eternally, I am grateful. Their stories are woven through the tough times that I narrated in this book. Without those loving people, I could not have made it. Like any mythological journey, I was lost in the thick forest, and found the talisman that cleared my way. The talisman for me was the powerful and palpable awareness that there are generous people who share love whether one "deserves" it or not.

The ancient myth of the phoenix lives in our collective mind because there is some truth about transformation inherent in the tale. Our personal stories either add to the collective battlefield, or contribute to the collective treaty.

Of course, the first move towards inner peace, instead of turmoil, requires an intention to possess it. Serenity can emerge from the ashes of any discord. As in my case, it can take a lengthy time. What's important is that inner strength can be developed from challenge.

Also, knowing adversity, I accepted that challenges would accompany me even after leaving home. Ever seeking more in life, I went on to have plenty of problems. While going through life's challenges, I felt like I was moving at a turtle's pace. Still I was moving.

Eventually, I made it to the experience of my power,

my peace and my strength.

What I decided in my early childhood was that I could not rely on anyone or anything. Deep down I thought that even God did not love me. As long as I was still alive, I had to rely on my puny strength. It was a depressing outlook.

Clear that I was profoundly unprepared for how life worked, I investigated and explored personal development classes, books, and audios. Relentlessly, I studied healthful emotional, mental and spiritual practices. While taking numerous transformational courses, seminars and workshops, I reached new perceptions and new perspectives. That pursuit led me to handling frequent pitfalls along the way. Each conflict, I met with endurance and fortitude. Expecting struggles, I was neither surprised nor slowed by them. As I overcame difficulties, I gradually learned to recognize and embrace my strengths that emerged out of the obstacles.

Everything I did took extreme physical and emotional effort. Constricted and restricted breathing was a metaphor for my limited experience of emotional nurturing. Still, neither stopped me from doing things. Everything I had to do, I did. Anything important that I wanted to do, I accomplished. Ever reaching for new goals, I continued to climb. I saw that my choice was to vegetate in a sea of stagnation or to struggle in the continuous challenges of life. Neither option looked appealing, but then life itself did not look attractive.

Distinguishing my abilities was my roadmap to emotional freedom. Friendships made all the difference with that.

PART ONE

THE FORMATIVE YEARS

BAD

Mother can be excused for considering me "trouble," a term she referred to me frequently. After all, her unusually docile firstborn was an idyllically behaved, beautiful blue-eyed blond son who never gave her a moment's worry. I was none of that. Reserved and quiet Jerry had misrepresented child behavior and Mother was unprepared for my vigor. When energetic Eddie came along, his charm won over Mother, and she accepted anything he did.

My parents told me that I was a jumper and a climber. Having no fear, I loved to leap from one place to another. When I was a year and a half old, I hopped from the crib to floor and broke my collarbone. Mother said I was "showing off" to my big brother.

When we were adults, Jerry told me that Mother beat me mercilessly for that. He appeared traumatized from the memory. Maybe it was not the fall that broke my collarbone, but the beating. Either way, I wore a cast for six months.

That experience must not have fazed me because at two years old I did it again. As soon as the cast came off, I jumped from one side of the alley to the other behind my house. There was a fence along both sides of the alley. There's no telling how I got over the fence to make that leap. The fall resulted in my other collarbone breaking and another six months in a cast. My shenanigans had to be frustrating to my parents.

Growing up, I heard other accounts of my toddler years, peppered with the words "trouble" and "bad."

There are no good stories of me as a child. One of the bad stories was that before I could walk, I managed to find a jar of mustard and smear it all over the kitchen floor. While I have no memory of that, I don't doubt that it happened, along with all the other stories of misdeeds my parents told of me.

THE ORPHANAGE

On a snowy December day, my parents gave me a present for my third birthday. My older brother Jerry received a present, too, since my birthday was combined with Christmas.

My folks informed us that they were taking Jerry and me away for a while. Furthermore, when we got back there would be a new child added to the family. My mother promised it would be a little sister for me, even though at that time, the gender could not possibly have been known until the baby's birth. Having a sister kindled some positive, though reluctant, anticipation. A sister would be a playmate, like a live doll, so I could see some benefits. Whether I liked it, or not, it was going to happen.

Still dismayed at the news, I sat in the back as my father drove my five-year-old brother and me to a strange, cold building with a dirty gray exterior. After a heavy door was opened, Jerry and I followed our father to a small room, where he handed an attendant a large paper bag that I hadn't noticed before. Dad told the lady that Jerry's and my clothes were in that brown paper grocery bag. After the shock of seeing my father hand over this connection to my life, I made it clear that I was unhappy and ready to leave.

The lady distracted Jerry and me. When I looked around my father was missing. Then, I clung to my brother whose brows were knit together and his jaw was tightly clenched. The attendant promised she would be right back as she led Jerry by the hand. When I followed, she stopped me, insisting that boys belong in another part of the building where girls were not allowed. Deeply distressed and hysterically fearful, I cried loudly as Jerry was taken away.

Stomping my feet, I then fell on the floor. My dramatics made no difference. Both my father and my brother were gone, and I was completely lost in an ocean of despair. When I recovered some time later, another uniformed attendant escorted me to a huge room where I encountered many cribs crammed with children. "Why are we stopping here?" I wondered, curious. Since it was the middle of the day, what were these children doing in a sleeping area? It reminded me of a zoo. Only here, the caged animals were children.

Resisting being placed in a crib like the other animals, I started again crying myself to exhaustion. Later, I awoke to the rattling of dishes. Food was being brought to the cribs. I did not want food, just freedom and family.

Gripped with fear and raging on at top speed as long as I could, I refused to relent to this foreign world. With every chance I got and with everyone who would listen, I demanded to see my brother, my one salvation and all that remained of the life I knew.

Hopelessly bereaved and with my whole body on fire, I was an inconsolable, bewildered soul. I did not care that my loud outbursts caused the other children discomfort.

Later, an attendant took off my clothes and shoes. I

assumed it was night. The windowless room gave me no clue. The first morning, I was issued a set of used, faded clothes. Told to hurry up and dress myself, I was too confused to move. I detested the unfamiliar, shabby clothes. They weren't mine. Indignant, I finally put them on reluctantly, complaining loudly that I wanted *my* clothes. I did not give up easily. Again and again, my serious complaints went unheeded. When one side of the crib was lowered, an attendant brought shoes to each child. The shoes I got were not the ones I took off the night before. The unfamiliar clothes bothered me, but not as much as the shoes. "Where did they go," I wondered. I had loved my brown and white shoes. They even had brown matching shoestrings, and I felt very proud when I wore them.

Quickly, I pointed out that someone had made a big mistake. When I decided to go barefoot, an attendant forced some disgusting shoes on my feet. Instead of mingling, I searched the room for who was wearing my precious shoes. Unable to find them, I thought they must be lost, like me. Nothing made sense. Nothing was right.

As days passed, slowly I realized that these children received different clothes everyday, none of which belong to anyone in particular. Horrified, I couldn't accept this repugnant way of life. I wanted nothing to do with these people, or this place.

At some point, in an effort to restore peace and quiet to my endless howls for my brother, an attendant allowed me a brief visit with Jerry. Different attendants brought us each into a hallway. Appearing to me as an ice statue, a faint resemblance of my brother, Jerry was a fellow prisoner of war. Hoping for a hug of solace and comfort from him, I stopped in my tracts. Seeing his dazed and bewildered countenance, Jerry's numbness revealed anxiety. In that moment of shock at his lack of reaction, I realized it was not that he had experienced missing me as I had him, but that he had been fearfully frozen about why he had been placed there. If there was anything in his blank face, it was apparent apprehension as to what was next. Had he grasped the gravity of the situation? He had lost any outrage, if indeed he ever had it. I wanted to shake him alive. Maybe he knew that he couldn't stay with me. Maybe he feared that reconnecting, only to leave again, would be too painful. I could not tell. More lost than I was, Jerry could neither express, nor connect.

It was then that I recognized I was on my own. We were two strangers on a train to the underworld. I took a good look at him with his hands in pants pockets, his drooping head of tousled hair, the stony silence in his eyes barely looking at me, all told me that we both were headed for new levels of hell.

My way of dealing with it was longing to hold on to a live connection with the known world. Escaping into himself was his way. We were both simply trying to survive.

Having given so much to make this meeting happen, I was prepared that this reunion might very well be our last in that place. It was. As I watched him being led away that day, I felt shivers of coldness. Knowing I was even more alone, more frustrated, and more brokenhearted than before was devastating. It was a lesson that willpower and determination do not always win the day.

The indignities continued incessantly. Not only sleeping in a crib, but also being assigned one in the daytime was offensive to me. Highly insulted, I knew that only babies were in cribs and I had outgrown that. Yet many of the other girls in cribs were bigger, if not older, than my three years.

After weeks of misery, too tired to voice my indignation, I looked around and wondered about my fellow inmates. "Where is their outcry?" I wondered. "How could they submit so easily?" I was suspicious of them. They couldn't be real children. They neither whimpered, nor complained. Unlike them, I was unable to be still. I wanted to run, jump and SCREAM all the time.

The huge room that was now my world was a pale gray. The same dull lifelessness permeated every- thing: the walls, the sheets, and the people. In this dreary existence, there was nothing to see and nothing to do. Toys were non-existent. There was no outside to view through windows. Doors were blocked. I hated the restrictions such as intolerable cribs and disheartening walls. For me, the building itself formed a giant, covered crib that I was trapped in.

There were plenty of other girls my age – girls with whom, theoretically, I could talk and commiserate. Others might have been supportive. I don't remember that. To me, everyone seemed very alone. There appeared to be no relationships that I could discern. The environment fostered separation. The walls of the crib would divide even twins. Looking around, I wondered if any of these girls had a sister, as I was expecting soon. Or was I going to have a sister? I didn't know if I could trust anything or anyone. No one could tell me when I could go home.

Feeling that I did not belong there, I just did not want to know anyone. I was not like them. Wanting to be disassociated, I told myself that I was not really an orphan. After all, I had parents, a house, a brother, and clothes that belonged to me. Choosing isolation was hard for me, but I could not afford to like these children. Besides, I figured that I would be out of there quickly. This minute would not be too soon. The next minute was not soon enough.

Time stood still in this hopeless place. "Will I ever get home again?" I worried and whimpered. It became evident that there was no point wasting my breath crying. No one heard and no one cared. Nothing changed, no matter what I felt or what I wanted. Yet I could not completely stop. Just when I thought that my dishrag self was all wrung out of tears, I would start again at times. I hated it there. There was nothing to like and no one to whom I was willing to relate.

For what seemed a lifetime, I did not see my brother. I wanted to cry every time I thought of him. So used to seeing these lonely kids, I wondered if I would even recognize him in the crowd of strangers. But I wanted him with me and nothing I did brought him close.

During those months, there was another day that stood out. An attendant I had never seen came to get me. "Wow," I thought, "I must be special. Maybe I am going home." This lady smiled brightly. Instantly I trusted her as she took me by the hand. We walked to a far off place where I had not been before.

Friendlier than the other adults, she disarmed me as I warmed up to her. Gently and humanely talking to me, she began undressing me when we got to a tiled room. Before I knew what was happening, I was alone, naked, and cold in a shower stall. Having experienced bathing only in a tub and never having had a shower, I did not understand what was happening. The woman stood outside the tiny room she put me in. "Why was she doing this?" Too terrified to speak or cry, I speculated to myself: "Is this the end of everything? Is this what it all has come to?" Suddenly, water cascaded down upon me. I screamed in shock, both from the coldness and the suddenness.

The attendant helped me dry off and dress myself, reassuring me that everything was all right. After walking me back to the large room where all the girls were, she disappeared.

After four months, seemingly a lifetime, my father came. Relieved and yet subdued, I felt like one emerging from a crypt. Arriving home, my freedom was only marred by the shock that there was no little sister. Worse, there was an annoying baby brother instead. It was Eddie who displaced the dream sister.

Again I was dismayed, distraught, and disappointed. If ever I had thought for a moment that my mother was omnipotent, it was gone forever. "How could she tell me something so essential as if it were fact, when she did not know for sure? Didn't she know how important this was to me? Maybe there was some mistake and it could all be cleared up."

As far as anyone could tell, Jerry was unmoved by the new brother. Still longing for that missing sister, I spent my early years hoping that she would show up, as long as I didn't have to go back to the orphanage.

Mother's explanation about that time period was that her doctor had warned her after I was born that she would die if she had a third child. The obstetrician probably knew that she wasn't emotionally strong enough to raise the two she had. Since she was Catholic, she proudly had a third pregnancy anyway, despite the threat to her life. Mother needed rest before her third child was born, so that explains why Jerry and I were sent to the orphanage. Dad had to work.

Jerry and I are now in our sixties, and we have never shared about this. While I have asked about what he remembers of that experience, he seems to have the memory locked in a vault in a very dark room that he has no wish to access.

Of course, I came to love my baby brother. And my dream of a sister has transformed. I have found my sister in the dazzling love from magnanimous, close friends around me. I experience my dream sister's essence in the beauty of nature, in the expansiveness of the oceans, in the mystery of the butterfly, in the sound of a bird, in the height of a mountaintop, and the movement of the clouds. Blessed and satisfied, I have my sister in every conversation with a loved one.

FAMILY LIES

In my family the lie was that everything in our family and home was normal. We were the good guys. Once, a neighbor lady yelled at someone else's pre-teen. My parents labeled that neighbor as crazy. My parents acted smug that we were better than the neighbor was. Even at the time, I had moments realizing how ironic that was. As a witness to my mother's mean behavior to other children, as well as her own, I knew better. Still, I wanted to believe the lie. It was too hard to admit the reality.

Despite the deep denial that anything was different in our family, secrecy abounded since we all knew our life was a mess and hiding it was a necessity. When we went to visit relatives, neighbors or friends, we were schooled in what not to say. It was not presented as protecting my parents from embarrassment. Rather, we were taught that others were busybodies and it was none of their business. We were saving others from their folly. We children obeyed since we needed some pride. The outside world protected the lie, too. Church members, neighbors and relatives ignored Mother's inappropriate actions and words as if it was not happening. No one spoke up about Mother's super loud singing. They ignored her nasty outbursts when other people's toddlers, bored with the long Mass Service, moved around the pew. In public places where my mother was not known and the social structure did not demand tolerance, there was often a backlash from others. In such instances, Mother acted like the victim of someone else's attack.

One example is when I was a preschooler, our family went into a buffet restaurant. Our table had an extra chair. When a woman asked to use the extra chair for her table, Mother was furious grabbing the chair as if she bought it herself. The woman grabbed the chair and there was a public tug of war. A worker intervened, and Mother fought with him. When she eventually lost the battle she yelled curses through her tears across the loud restaurant. Mother did not need the chair. It was all about winning.

Dad did not move during the long siege, but he comforted her afterwards. Unable to eat after all that drama, I wanted to leave. Mother was all stirred up and I knew I'd be the outlet of her rage.

QUASIMODO

Beginning before my first birthday, my parents noticed that I had trouble breathing. Asthma was the label for me. Asthmatic bronchitis was the label for my two brothers.

It is quite possible that the signs were there even before my first birthday. The air in the house was cold and damp in the winter with the heat vent on the ceiling. Heat rises, so we did not feel warm air. Hot and sticky air ruled the summer, since our parents thought that a window air conditioner cost too much. When I moved out they decided to get one. Go figure.

Breathing was harder for me than anyone I knew. Since I would hunch over trying to compensate for the pain of breathing, I felt like Quasimodo. the Hunchback of Notre Dame. As long as I can remember, my father told me I was 'barrel-chested.'

Looking down was natural for me. Doctors had no answers for my breathing problems, only potions of foul tasting liquid medicine that made me feel worse. When other children got colds, I got pneumonia. I was seen as deficient, even though I compensated by being as active as anyone, and more than most.

In school, I was scolded for "not standing up straight." Evidently, teachers thought that I was choosing to frustrate them. I felt guilty. Instead of getting needed medical help, I was chastised for coughing repeatedly. Constantly, I worried about bothering others with my noisy coughing, and I feared the next cough that could happen any moment. Diligently, I practiced suppressing the cough. In the process, suppression eventually led to more blocked airways.

In grade school, my coughing bothered a nun who frequently ordered me to stand outside the classroom. She scolded me while I was still holding on to the desk to support my breathing. I had to stand up for hours and the only support was the corridor wall. It was the wall of shame for being put out. Anyone walking by stared at my rounded posture as I tried to compensate for not getting enough air.

By high school, I got used to coughing up blood at times. I didn't worry about it since I didn't know what could be done. There was no point thinking about what I couldn't control.

At age 14, I was diagnosed with emphysema and spent a month in a hospital with doctors who had no hope for me. In college at 17, a doctor predicted that I would not live to see my 25th birthday. Since he had no solution for me, I ignored the prediction. In my twenties, I was treated for TB. Later, the problem was called bronchiectasis, an abnormal stretching and enlarging of the respiratory passages. That was followed in my forties by an inaccurate diagnosis of lung cancer.

Fortunately, I chose not to have lung surgery that the pulmonologist strongly urged. When I got a second medical opinion about the surgery, another pulmonologist said that the surgery could kill me, so I might as well go the easy route and do nothing. It worked for me.

My extreme lung condition was inexplicable. My parents smoked Lucky Strikes everyday, but most parents smoked and their children did not suffer to the extent I did. When scars and air pockets were found throughout my lungs, there was no medical explanation. I never smoked. And I did not have the known gene for lung abnormalities.

Recently, I decided that I must be an anomaly. While the medical establishment can learn from an anomaly, they are not interested. My present pulmonologist says she thinks it is likely that I had end stage asthma when I was diagnosed with emphysema at age 14. The average person lives only ten years with end stage asthma.

Whenever I had trouble breathing, I wanted to hide. I always went to my bedroom to be alone with the shades down. This, along with all my behavior, annoyed my mother. At the time, I could not explain my hiding, even to myself.

On one memorable day, my mother harassed me incessantly when hiding in my bedroom. She said that I would breathe better outside in the "fresh air." I was not so sure. Insisting I do obey, she told me she was bringing a chair to the patio out back. For sure I was not in favor of this idea. My reluctance and resistance revolved around the real fear that if I did not feel any better outside, that meant a challenging climb back up two sets of steps to my bedroom. I knew it was a monumental risk that was unlikely to go well for me. Yet, Mother was adamant and persisted like a toddler repeating "why" over and over without listening to the answer.

At four years old, I was no match for Mother's tactics.

She didn't stop shouting, so there was no peace without doing her bidding. Just the sound of her voice stirred anxiety that made it harder to breathe. I relented. Slowly, I submitted to her demands. And after all, I thought: "She is doing it for me."

As soon as I tried to sit a bit comfortably in the fold-up chair, I leaned on the shaky chair arms and held on for dear life. I needed the chair arms to support me. Then wordlessly my mother went back into the house.

Looking around at the gate, I wistfully thought of what the gate meant to me. I remembered how I learned to escape the confines of the yard. Older brother Jerry had showed me how he climbed over the fence. Too short for that, I put my hand through the slats and discovered I could unhook the lock from the other side. No fuss, no problem. Then I locked the gate behind me.

Mother caught me frequently. Never liking my adventures, she would beat me, but the longing for a wider world was worth the price. The beatings never stopped me. And I was emboldened by the fact that she didn't catch me all the time.

Coming back to where I was in the chair, I thought: "I'd be out of the gate now if I could breathe." Dad had recently built a sandbox on the far side of the small concrete yard. He hoped that Jerry and I would be inclined to stay in that space. Eddie was still a baby. Later he would slide under the gate to freedom. When he got out, Mother never got upset.

Somehow the sandbox didn't have the same attraction as the neighborhood. All the kids liked to see Mrs. Martin who gave kids a lollipop when they came to her door. I was no exception. Mrs. Martin lived down the block and it was a great motivator for me to get out, no matter what the consequences.

Since Mother knew how quickly I could vanish, I knew that I could not stay outside the gate for long. My strategy was to get out and back before she knew I was gone. Yet my sense of time was not good. There wasn't a person living on our street that I did not know by name. Still intending to be quick, if I saw anyone sitting on a porch, I couldn't stop myself from pausing to say hello, so as not to seem unfriendly.

Most often, I went to the train tracks two blocks away. While waiting for the train, I could hear the sound it made even when it was not there. The train whistles held excitement and longing. Puzzled as to where the train might be going, I couldn't imagine what was out beyond my neighborhood. My neighborhood was just one place the train went to as it passed through without stopping on its way to somewhere important. Thinking of that made me happy. For years after we moved from that place, I continued to hear the train sounds in my head and in my sleep, loud and clear. It was the only thing I missed from that original neighborhood, even more than Mrs. Martin's lollipops.

Interrupting my reverie of healthier days, just then a man came with Mother through the outside gate into the yard. Pointing to me, Mother stated: "This is my daughter. She is my cross to bear in life." Sighing, she informed him how hard I was for her.

It was a relief that the man was not someone who lived on our street. No telling where Mother found him. He was very old and very uncomfortable. Looking at me sadly, and shaking his head, he left quickly. As he moved out of sight, Mother continued to talk to him about what a burden I was.

Not breathing well enough to argue, I had nothing to say. It occurred to me that she was my cross, more than the other way. Though the scene was brief, I was humiliated. Knowing I had to keep my anger under wraps, I felt the boiling pot of burning resentment that had nowhere to go.

Many years later when I was a pre-teen, I was old enough to refuse her demands to sit outside. So one day she brought the mailman into my bedroom when I was struggling and hunched over trying to get the next breath. Solemnly, she clearly informed him that she was a good Christian and I was her thorny cross to bear. In no shape to pretend normalcy, having nothing more to lose and too immobilized to speak, I was consumed with rage covered over with resignation. So familiar with mortification, I told myself that I couldn't afford to care what any stranger thought.

That time, I was struck by the term *cross*, the religious symbol everywhere at school, church, and home. It was impossible to get away from it. Praying the Stations-of-the-Cross was a required ritual during Lent, the six-week penitential time in Catholic churches. Each year I had been exposed to suffocating strong incense that would gag a garbage truck driver. Whatever positive symbolism the cross represented, it was lost to me.

After that I longed to have a door lock to keep me safe. My pleadings to my father had no effect. Mother came in anytime. I had no semblance of protection, much less privacy.

THE BELOVED DOLL

At five, I was the big sister to a toddler brother. Accepting him took time, but after two years I was used to this intrusion. Inadvertently, his toenail got torn down to the flesh and he was crying in pain. Mother did not know what to do to fix the problem. I hugged him to stop the noise and tears.

Then I put him in the stroller and rode him around the tiny back yard as he whimpered loud enough to keep up the sympathy. Though it hadn't happened to me, I felt sorry for him.

The backyard was defined by a fence around the concrete that took me about thirty steps in any direction to get from one side to the far end of the other. Nevertheless, I took orders from him as I pulled him in his wagon around the little space.

It was this little brother with the big brown eyes, still in diapers, who took a liking to bashing my dolls on the concrete. Yes, more concrete in my life. Mother thought the doll bashing was cute and amusing.

Once, after my brother's cruelty to my doll, I cried. My heart was ripped open. Deriding me for crying, my mother proceeded to conduct a funeral ceremony for one abused, broken, favorite doll. My mother and baby brother merrily marched in a procession humming a dirge. I did not follow. It was all very clear to me that my pain had provided much entertainment.

If I ever saw that doll again it made no impression on my memory. I knew I couldn't be sure that the dolls that were left wouldn't become brother-damaged dolls too, but as long as I had them I would cherish them. What I took away that day was bigger than the doll. It was then that I saw the family circus for what it was. I was better prepared for the future.

As young as I was, I knew for sure that my younger brother was blameless. He only knew what he was taught. He would not hurt me without support.

THE LONE WINDOW

On Sundays, my parents told us that we children were going to a type of kindergarten school, while they were going to church. Open to something different, it did not take long to find it was worse than Mass.

Two teen girls tried desperately to control the three of us along with about 50 other pre-school children. Apparently their main goal was to keep us from leaving. To me, there seemed no reason to stay. Luckily, it was just once a week, but I dreaded this lock-up time.

Then one day, Jerry went off to first grade. He was late. Mother was not finished making him a sandwich. It was an effort. "This school must be an important experience," I figured. During the day, I wondered where Jerry was and what he was doing. Feeling left behind, left out, and left alone, I had less to occupy me with Jerry gone. Feeling deprived, I wished I could go, too.

Every day I awaited his return; in much the same way that Penelope, for twenty years, awaited Odysseus' reappearance from the Trojan Wars. Jerry's homecoming was an event for me, though he was usually not in a good mood. He had homework. Wanting to see the homework, I sought to do what he did. Mother gave me his assignment. She took a few minutes and showed me how to do it. I loved it. The only table that fitted me was the high chair that, of course, I had outgrown. The kitchen table was too high. I did not care where I wrote. With pencil in my hands and paper on some surface, I felt alive with purpose. Now I was BIG.

This scenario continued for the whole school year. Eagerly, I watched and anticipated Jerry's return in awe of his travels to a mysterious land. First grade seemed like a golden opportunity and I savored the time to just imagine what it would be like.

At last, the first day of school came like a gift from heaven. I was completely enthralled. Things were frantic with both Jerry and me trying to get out in time. While it was a mile-long walk, Jerry did not leave me completely behind, though his legs were longer and quicker. I was grateful, though out of breath from running just to keep up. It was a sunny September morning. There were many streets we had to cross. Since school was next to church, I knew the way. Arriving at the schoolyard, I marveled at all the children, never having seen so many in one place.

Then a bell rang and Jerry started to leave me. Noticing this, I started to follow. A nun grabbed me and pointed me to a tiny building rather than the big school where Jerry was heading. The small building was the annex. Under the shiny bright sky, I liked being outside. Yet the anticipation of the new school life called me inside.

While a little portion of the annex was above ground, the only entrance was down dark, stone steps. It seemed like I was disappearing into a dungeon. Only two rooms were in this basement. Both rooms were for first graders. Feeling a chill, I was keenly aware of the loss of light. Never before had I taken such notice of the stark, sudden contrast between light outside and dark inside. Jerry was not one to prepare me for this, or any changes. Now after wanting this school thing so much, I was already uneasy, and looking forward to being a second grader in the big building above ground.

Finding my way to the classroom, I looked around and saw no one that I knew. My friend up the street did not attend Catholic school.

The teacher, a friendly but stern nun, did her best to keep my attention. Yet my mind was on the only window, located near the ceiling. It was a small space that was slightly above ground with heavy bars across it. Though the bars were disturbing, that one window was my salvation. It made me feel connected to the rest of life. The sun was still shining even if could not shine directly in this window at pavement level. It felt comforting to know I would be free and out there sometime that day. It intrigued me to think about what others were doing each day while I was hidden away in this place.

Though it was hard coming inside after a short recess, I decided I was glad I was in school. The day went fast. I loved the familiar world of letters, words, and numbers that first I saw through Jerry's homework. More and more opened up before me. There were others enclosed with me, people to get to know. There were things to learn. And there was no Mother.

CRIME AND PUNISHMENT

After the first few school months that year, I heard children saying that one child had been bad. Not knowing who it was, I was just glad it wasn't me, at least not yet.

Teachers warned us repeatedly that bad behavior resulted in being taken to the convent where there was a dungeon for naughty children. Seeing the window bars in the classroom, I could readily believe that. I understood that the nun policing the play yard really was a warden. All of us were under scrutiny as potential criminals.

That same day, children milling around the schoolyard told me about the dungeon. The weather was cold outside already and I suspected that the dungeon was not heated. Searching for Jerry, I went scurrying home. I vowed to avoid bad behavior, or at least to avoid getting caught. Knowing myself, I recognized that escaping apprehension was my only hope, and a slim one at that.

HOW ICE CREAM CAN GO WRONG

Three-year-old Eddie was shuffled off to stay with a neighbor family as Jerry and I piled into the back of the car. My parents wanted to look at houses in a new suburb outside of Philadelphia. For me, it was a ho-hum time looking at humdrum houses. I was not looking forward to the hot ride there and back in a crowded car with nothing to do.

In one house, a woman said my hair was pretty. Mother had said that if I ate a pound of carrots, then my hair would curl. In other words, then my hair would be acceptable. So hearing that my straight hair was pretty because it had red highlights, I was very pleasantly surprised. So it was not such a bad day.

Stopping at a roadside restaurant, Dad announced that we could have a snack before making the trip back home. I was amazed and ecstatic. What a rare treat! In fact, this was the first time that I ever remembered such an experience. At six, I was sure of it.

On that sunny, humid day at this restaurant, my parents made dessert choices for themselves. At a table outside, we waited for their order to arrive. Feeling a breeze and sitting in some shade, I thought that this day had really taken a turn for the better.

Arriving with a tray, a waitress with a white apron placed in front of my parents the stemmed glass bowls filled with the delectable frozen feast. In front of Jerry and me, she set the empty plates. I looked at Mother for what would end up in my bowl. I liked chocolate. Vanilla was boring. Strawberry was just plain wrong. Mother knew my preferences. I got strawberry.

When the scoop landed on our plates from my parents' overflowing bowls, I noticed that Jerry's was twice the size of mine. I protested. Mother was adamant in her explanation. Jerry was older by more than a year. Somehow I knew that his scoop was greater than the difference in our age. Sure that this discrepancy had to do with the size of the partiality, I was not buying the ridiculous reason. I didn't even like the flavor, but I wanted my share. Utterly inconsolable, I ate the ice cream only to avoid the guilt of being called ungrateful, something I knew I was demonstrating. Thinking that I was a miserable brat, I did not enjoy the eventual melted ice cream one bit. Surely, no one enjoyed theirs either. No one had any joy except possibly Jerry, who likely reveled in the preferential treatment, his moment in the sun.

HIDDEN NURTURANCE

That summer, I was age six and finished first grade and the annex school. My family moved from Philadelphia to the suburbs about thirty miles west of our old row house. Occasionally, Mother spoke of Naomi and how wonderful she was. That was rare to hear anything good about anyone, unless they were a priest, a doctor, or the pope. Naomi was a hired housekeeper that helped Mother with Jerry and me in the other house. "She took care of you two," Mother said. "I wish that I could remember," I thought. It had to have been when I was an infant.

Ordinarily, Mother mentioned Naomi while comparing her to the more recent housekeeper who was "not worth anything." Often Mother mocked each succeeding housekeeper behind her back. No one lasted long. No one on earth pleased my mother, it appeared.

While living in a row house in West Philadelphia, we did not have a lot of money. Evidently Dad was willing to spend the little we had on housekeeping to take pressure off Mother. From the piles of rumpled clothes on the floor and dirty dishes filling the sink, it was clear that housekeeping completely overwhelmed her.

After moving to the suburbs, Mother wanted to go back to the city to see Naomi, whom she hadn't seen in many years. Clearly, Mother had missed Naomi. Not knowing why Naomi left, I dared not ask.

All five of us drove to the all black neighborhood and walked up the steep, broken steps to her row home on a narrow street. Naomi got to meet our youngest family member, now three years old, for the first time. Warm and friendly, Naomi hugged me tight and I felt like I was melting into her ample flesh. I was glad she knew me, though felt at a disadvantage not knowing her. With great kindness, she brought us something to drink along with cookies.

After we left that day, Mother still spoke of Naomi. It was as if Naomi was an unreachable concept. As far as I know there were no more phone calls. It is likely that Mother at some earlier point offended Naomi, who took leave in self-defense. Possibly Naomi realized that Mother was too hotheaded to handle.

Naomi was a generous person who may have forgiven Mother enough to meet with us, but not enough to communicate beyond that. It was sad for Mother that the two did not meet again. Surprisingly, Mother was aware enough to be grateful to her and to admit that Naomi genuinely contributed to our family.

It must have been Naomi's love that made my mother grateful. Naomi's housekeeping never meant much to Mother. She preferred a mess. Refusing to have a housekeeper in the suburb, Dad became habituated to the messiness that escalated exponentially by the year.

MY HOMEWORK AND A BOY'S

No longer did I walk a mile to school in all kinds of weather. Here in second grade, the bus came a half block away. That meant a lot to me.

Since Dad had happy memories of growing up on a farm with his parents and eight siblings, he wanted this house to have a grassy yard where Dad could plant a modest vegetable garden in the back. A nature lover, Dad as a young adult rented a farm with two of his brothers before he married.

Mother did not share Dad's farm passion since she was raised a city girl who grew up in Philadelphia with 3 siblings, a seamstress homemaker mother and a county club manager father whose drinking squandered most of his earnings. Since both Dad and Mother's parents died before I was born, I didn't know my grandparents.

For Mother, the suburbs may have seemed a foreign land, far from the city. Nor was it a perfect fit for Dad, obviously for different reasons. It was one place where they compromised, neither getting exactly what they wanted.

Just before school one morning, Mother called me to her bed where she was sitting up. She had found my homework and was very upset with the date on my paper. Distressed, she pointed out that on Thursday I had written the date for Friday. That meant that this day was the end of the world. She assumed I was prophetic, that somehow I knew ahead of time that this was the day. I assured her that my teacher required all her students to write the date the homework was due, not the day it was done. Not satisfied with my explanation, Mother insisted that this homework page was a sign from God. I was sure that I did not explain it right.

An early spring day, it was too nice a day for the end of world, I reasoned. Jerry and I were all ready for school. Pleading for my homework, I suggested that I could make it to the bus up the street if I left right away. Since we were never ready on time, I always got out of breath running to catch the bus.

Refusing to let the paper go, Mother repeated over and over that: "The end is today." That was what the homework meant, she pointed out. Dad let Jerry leave for school, but Mother wanted me to stay. Very sure that somehow I must be responsible for creating this upset, I felt profoundly culpable for the confusion.

Mother wanted to go out and warn the world about the impending doom. Dad took little Eddie to stay with a neighbor. We drove around for a few hours. Finally Dad stopped in our church parking lot. Instead of going into the church, he walked up to Father Kelley's rectory. Knocking on the door, he waited until the pastor's housekeeper opened it.

Besides being the pastor, Father Kelley was the school principal. Many times he had come around to the classrooms. It was always nice to see him. Every Sunday, I saw him say Mass. So impressed with him, my parents considered the priest to be the most important person in the community. He had been to our house the week before, sitting down talking about our family obligation to contribute money for parish support and for our expenses at the school. Respecting him, I admired all he represented. There was no one I knew that was more esteemed.

Dad spoke to Fr. Kelley for a minute. Then he signaled for Mother and me to enter. My parents talked in another room while I waited alone in the foyer. Even the housekeeper left me alone as I wondered what was going on. "Maybe that woman knew that it was my fault," I pondered. "Maybe Father Kelley could convince Mother that it really it is not the time for the end of the world. But what if she was right? Maybe she would convince him since she was very good at that." I hoped that it was not the end since I was not ready for that. I would have missed my classmates and my teacher, Sister Marie Charles.

My teacher treated me as though she thought I was smart. Mother explained to me that the teacher was mistaken. I was not really intelligent at all. She told me that I just went to first grade in a school that had more advanced teaching than this new school, so that's why I knew more than others in second grade. I prayed that my teacher would not find out why school was easy for me. So young, I was already a fraud.

Interrupting my thoughts, Dad and Mother came out of Father's office as Father walked us to the front door. He told them that God was in charge and everything was going to be fine. Somehow I did not think he believed what he said. Never had I seen him look so serious. He did not look at me. Fr. Kelley did not tell my parents I should have been in school. Saying goodbye, he closed the door quickly as if he had more pressing concerns.

Despite the good Father's assuring words about God being in charge, I felt sick in the pit of my stomach. Since there was no higher place to go in our world than to Father Kelley, there was no hope. "Did he think Mother could be right and is making preparations for himself right now?" I wondered. I felt alone and lost. "Would I ever go to school again?" It was hard to be really afraid of the end of the world since I couldn't imagine it. I just longed to survive whatever was going to happen next, since even Fr. Kelley had no remedy for Mother's rambling.

More thoughts kept racing as we walked the short distance to the car: "What if Mother never wants to go home? What if we spend our lives on the road as we had for hours?" Thinking of all that, made me more afraid than the end of the world idea. This world had not been too great Truly, I was not so worried about that.

Getting in the backseat of the car, I knew we were going in circles. I was caught in the middle. There were no answers. Mother was upset while Dad followed her aimless lead. Dad's face revealed nothing. The more he listened to her shout directions, the more frantic Mother got. Oh how I wished I could have gone to school that day. Too scared of being lost forever on the highway, I could not cry. Knowing what would come next, would not have made me better off. What happened later that day, I have never forgotten.

We drove for what seemed an endless nightmare, a lengthy time doing only what Mother wanted. "Turn left. Now go right," Mother shrilled to my father, instructing him when to stop, when to go, when to slow down and when to speed up. No one knew where we were headed. Gradually I realized that Dad did not know how to get back home.

While I needed a bathroom, I was hungry, too. I said nothing. Though Dad was the driver, Mother had the power. In our family, Mother's desires were always the only consideration. I knew I could wait out any discomfort. Even at home, Mother would chase me out of the bathroom if she wanted to use the toilet, especially if I was on it. It happened quite frequently. No place was ever safe.

After more time driving everywhere, Mother's wild direction led us to a farming area. Annoyed, Dad started to complain that he had never seen the area before. Silently, I could not shake the fear that the intensely antagonistic, inescapable ride would never be over.

Suddenly, Mother was hungry and there were no restaurants around. She got angrier by the minute. Whenever she was hungry, it was a major crisis that had to be handled instantaneously. Now it was all Dad's fault that we were lost.

Commanding Dad to stop at a house, Mother led the way up to the door. A boy my age answered the doorbell. Mother told him she wanted food as she pushed her way inside. Dad and I followed. There was no adult there.

Extremely uncomfortable, the boy looked bewildered. As Mother went through the refrigerator, I shyly asked the nervous wide-eyed boy his name and why he wasn't in school. "Steve" he responded. He said that he went to school and it was over for the day. It was 4 PM already. While he continued repeating that his parents would be home soon, Mother was not intimidated.

Despite Mother's confidence, I wanted to get out of there before anyone else arrived. Mother had found some apples that she was happily biting into. There were some cheese slices, so she helped herself. Though famished, I would not partake. Continuing to look for more food, Mother found some homemade cupcakes in the breadbox. Steve tearfully informed her that the desserts were for after dinner and definitely off limits. He was not allowed to touch them. His predicament was OK with Mother who was already munching on one of the treats. I felt that I was part of a heist. Steve was visibly shaken.

Just then Mother spotted a notebook and picked it up. She told Steve that she needed it. He bravely found his voice and strongly let her know that he required the notebook, since all his homework was in it. Oh, I knew this was a mistake to let Mother know any personal needs. Trying desperately to defend himself, Steve could not have known Mother's perversity.

Mother asserted that she was keeping it. As Steve begged her to give it back, Mother clutched the food that she had taken and ran out of the house with the notebook under her arm.

Looking at Dad, my eyes fill up with emotion. Feeling sad for Steve, I weakly stammered out: "He needs it for school. He'll be in trouble. The notebook belongs to him. Steve would need to study with that notebook."

Dad ignored me. I thought that I had not spoken up enough for this boy. No one understood like I did. "How could I make Dad understand? How could Dad not know what will happen?"

I knew that no one would ever believe Steve's story. Even Steve won't believe that this could be true. He would think he had dreamt this incident. The nightmare for him would continue when his parents accused him of eating the food and losing the homework book. The anguish would follow this innocent boy as his teacher blamed him for the lost notebook with his whole year's class notes and homework.

Torn, I wanted to stay and defend Steve when his parents came. Turning, I saw the boy at the door with his tortured face still begging for the notebook. I knew exactly what he felt. As we got in the car, my heart was shattered into little chards. I had let a terrible thing happen. I had been there and had not been effective in interceding.

After a long time, Dad found the way home somehow. Mother was winding down since it was her usual naptime before dinner. Jerry had been waiting at the doorstep for hours since the school bus left him off. Dad walked to the neighbor's to get Eddie. We were back in the house, but it all seemed different. Nothing was ever the same for me again.

As I went to bed after dark, I remembered that the day was not over. There were a few hours left. That day was in some way an end of the world for me. I had witnessed a very dark side of the world. That boy's pleading screams rang in my ears. I saw the helplessness on his face. I hear and see him still.

THE AFTERMATH OF ONE PSYCHOTIC EPISODE

Some weeks after that end-of-the-world episode, my mother went to a mental hospital. That would be the first of many times that I knew of.

As a six year old, I was still grieving over my mother's wild delusions and my father's helpless indecision. My inner messages of automatic self-blame made it worse. I feared that if I inadvertently said or wrote something, my mother would become more bizarre. Illogically, I felt that there might be some hidden rule that unknowingly I could violate. Like my homework with the due date on it, I might trigger my mother's erratic behavior again.

Dad's passive tolerance allowed the situation to careen out of control, causing emotional pain to a young boy. Yet, I knew it as my fault.

Whatever directly led to Mother's hospitalization was unclear to me. Things must have gotten worse. What I did know was that while Mother was away, each of us children was sent to different relatives.

Still in second grade, I went to live with my father's brother Joe, and Uncle Joe's wife Betty, who treated me kindly. Though I didn't miss my home, I missed my school friends and familiar school environment. While there, I was placed in a very slow class in an unfamiliar school. Bored silly, I despised it.

After awhile, I was transferred to yet another second grade in the same school. It was a better fit educationally, but it was one more set of people and I missed my real friends back home more acutely. Though I loved my aunt and uncle and my two boy cousins, after several months I was feeling terribly unsettled. Not knowing when, if ever, I'd be going home, I felt profoundly sad at this new layer of instability, having to adjust to so many changes.

One Friday, I told the teacher that I wasn't coming back after the weekend. I meant it. I was ready to run away if necessary. Somehow changes occurred and I don't know if it was coincidental.

Possibly I told my Aunt Betty or maybe the school contacted her. A practical woman of action, Aunt Betty made things happen. That weekend, I was sent home where my mother had already returned from the mental hospital ward.

STEW

The old fairy tale, *Stone Soup* is a delight. It tells of a clever soldier who tricked poor townspeople into feeding him by suggesting that his 'magical' stone could feed everyone. Every townsperson was enrolled in adding some food to the stone at the bottom of a huge pot of boiling water. Yep, just a common stone started a wondrous feast of sharing. The whole community was fed, including the hungry soldier traveling through town. I love that fiction.

Looking back, I wish I had known about that story when I was eating grass soup on a regular basis. My mother generally added nothing to the boiled water and grass except her insistence that she worked all day to cook it. A family staple, grass soup happened quite often, even in the winter when grass was not growing. The yard just looked bald after Mother pulled up remaining dead grass.

Dad would get angry with us for complaining that there was nothing substantial in the bad tasting boiled water with the floating grass.

On some lucky days there would be some ham bones or chicken bones mixed in. On those days, I could never remember having recently eaten ham or chicken that could have resulted in leftover bones.

Whoever ate the original meat on the bone was a mystery to me. Knowing Mother's penchant for going through neighbors' garbage, I didn't want to know for sure where she got those bones.

"You're strange," Dad would say critically to my daring younger brother who objected most loudly. It was wrong to be different.

Though we were on familiar terms with the soup, the sheer repetition made it more upsetting. Fearing rebellion, Dad directed his message to all of us.

Knowing that Dad was eating it too, I wondered how he could chastise us with a straight face. He never let on. I suspect that he ate before he came home. He was not as skinny as we were.

When allergy tests revealed that I was allergic to grass, still nothing changed. Grass soup ruled. It was not called that, of course. It was called stew.

Later as an adult, a friend said she was fixing stew for dinner. I was shocked that anyone would admit to cooking that. I had to remind myself that it couldn't be the same thing that I had eaten on a regular basis.

I'LL GET IT RIGHT AWAY

With her barbwire personality, even Mother's "hello" had an edge to it. The mantra in the house was: "Where's the silverware? Where is a plate? Where are the drinking glasses? Where's the toothpaste? Where are the towels? Where are my schoolbooks that I just left by the chair?" The specific question didn't matter. Whatever it was, the missing item could be anywhere. Mother enjoyed 'putting things away' so they could not be found.

The towels were never in the linen closet and dishes were not stored in the kitchen. That would be a mistake to expect that anything would be in a convenient place. Nothing was in the same place two days in a row. If you put it where it was suitable for you, then you could be certain it would not stay there, since Mother reveled in chaos like a ravenous dog revels in a garbage dump.

To our mantra: "Where is _____?" said to oneself and not to anyone in particular, Mother's mantra was: "Oh, I'll go get it for you right away," delivered with heavy measure of sarcasm.

The unspoken message was: "How stupid of you to ask." Then the laugh would begin, just in case you missed the point that your needs were a joke. In this, Mother was an equal opportunity mother. My brothers received no special treatment either.

Searches were never-ending. No day was easy. For

example, no matter how long it took to get clean in a bath or shower, it took ten times longer to take stuff out of the tub first. Filled to the top, it was always piled with dozens of inexplicable things. At anytime on any day, they were different items. No matter, it was always packed. Outside of the tub, the rest of the bathroom was too small to hold all those obstacles to bathing, so we had to distribute the contents in other rooms before getting into the filthy tub.

In the living room, the one phone often was missing. It had a very long cord that could go in all directions spanning three rooms. It always got lost under huge piles of junk. I could hear it when it rang, but only a general direction. Removing the debris was a tougher problem.

The searches for any items were trickier than a scavenger hunt without any clues. Whatever you were looking for really could be anywhere. It could be in the back of a shelf hidden behind numerous other items, stuffed in a drawer, wedged behind or under furniture, etc. There were no boundaries. Some usual places to find things included the bottom of the hallow chair, which itself could be anyplace. Or, another favorite hideaway for household items was between the mattress and the exposed springs of any bed. That was no easy task for me to lift the heavy mattress.

A lost item could be under a sink behind the drain. It might be in the center of the tub underneath the piles of mishmash. Many things were broken, because of the weight of the things on top. Or you might find the missing item under or behind the heater. But those were the regular spots and only about 10% of the time those were feasible. Something would be in those places, but not necessarily the object of the hunt.

Hard to reach places were Mother's specialties.

Perpetually, no matter how clever your search, Mother was a few steps ahead. If you were dumb enough to ask her why that particular place, she would have a meaningless justification. No one past five years old ever asked. It was a waste of breath.

Mother even confounded herself. Rarely could she find anything she wanted either.

St. Jude, the patron of lost items, was the saint to whom we prayed. Working overtime in our house, St. Jude was not effective in the least. He didn't have time for our family, apparently. That didn't stop Mother from praying.

WHO DO YOU THINK YOU ARE!

Mother had a plentitude of ways of keeping me feeling insignificant. One was to consistently tell me to eat carrots since that would make my straight hair curl. Hardly ever did we have carrots in the house. Also, she would tell me that the **only** thing I had going for my looks was my hair.

Dad had his belittling tactics, too. Regularly he would say: "Who do you think you are?" It was not a question, but rather a rhetorical statement, often directed at Eddie.

Somehow Eddie had the audacious notion that he was important. Furthermore, he stood up for that dignity. I admired that, but couldn't find worth or value within me. Knowing the reprisals from Dad, I might not have declared my value if I had it to proclaim.

Dad did not like the idea that anyone would think highly of oneself. He considered it wrong to think that way. He and Mother often mocked neighbors, judging them as 'haughty-taughty.' We children were warned about other children or adults who were "full of themselves."

There were frequent confrontations between Eddie and Dad. Eddie banged doors, talking back to defend himself. Mother forgave everything. Dad reacted harshly. Since overtly Eddie did not win any battles and Dad was the 'victor,' the drama was a cautionary tale for me. The message was clear.

Despite his domination of us, Dad had many admirable traits. I looked up to him. Every weekday morning he would get ready for work and go off to a great job. Responsible with steady commitment, he left and returned effortlessly. I was impressed that Dad knew how to get places and knew how to fix things.

Dad had the good fortune to leave the house, even in the summer when the rest of us had to stay home and deal with Mother. When I expressed my pride in his engineering job and suggested that he was valuable at work, he told me that anyone could be replaced at a moment's notice. I felt depressed with this piece of news because I was sure that Dad could not be replaced anywhere. He lived his question: "Who do you think you are?"

FAMILY UN-TOGETHERNESS

At home, Dad delighted in the thought of saving money by making a homemade version of ice cream. As far as I could tell, he was not interested in the health benefits. Saving money was everything.

It took the better part of a day using his new equipment. We three children each took turns churning and wondering how to avoid the boring hard work. Mother's aversion to work made it acceptable that she was not expected to help. We knew she was the exception to the working part of the ice cream project.

At first the novelty of mixing the ingredients in the machine made it somewhat bearable. That didn't last long. Dad did his version of trying to sell us on the joys of hand mixing ice cream. We had read Tom Sawyer and were not like the gullible friends who whitewashed Tom's fence for him. Dad did not have Tom Sawyer's success. We didn't buy the hype.

After long hard hours of tedious labor with each of us begrudgingly working for a while, the result actually tasted surprisingly good. It had a maple flavor, which I thought was weird for ice cream. Besides melting swiftly, there was little that was recognizable by any store bought standard. It lost my interest since it was not chocolate.

The next part was the real crowning glory. Mother poured large heaps of wheat germ all over the fast melting ice cream before we could eat it. The bitter flakes overwhelmed the taste of the ice cream. It ended up being more like wheat germ cereal with a little maple sweet milk.

After that first time, none of us kids ever really thought that homemade ice cream was worth the effort. Store bought ice cream remained unknown in our house for a long time. Dad continued his attempts to entice us into his ice cream project. In order to please, I would occasionally agree to go along with the effort. Soon, I joined my brothers finding urgent reasons why I couldn't do the churning. Soon, the ice cream maker occupied space in a kitchen corner as a symbol of our obstinacy.

CHRISTMAS DECORATIONS

"Merry Christmas, Munchkin" my friends screamed as we scattered like leaves in the December wind, all going our separate ways. At age twelve, I went to Girl Scout meetings directly after school on Tuesdays.

The setting sun was having a fascinating dance with the clouds. It looked like the aftermath of a horde of chickens whose feet ran through spilled pink and orange paint tracking it across the sky.

Soon noticing the sky darkening, I was looking forward to being warmer, not having been home since early morning. Pulling my collar up to brace the gale force winds against my face, I dreaded the mile long walk I had to travel as the daylight was dying rapidly. Feeling the loss of the sun, I was alone on this bitter cold night., despite the well lit homes I passed along the way.

Suddenly, a boy approached. To my amazement, it was my 13-year-old brother. "Hi Jerry," I exclaimed a bit more excitedly than I wanted to let on. He said nothing as he approached. Abruptly, he turned down the street that was not on the way home. "Wanna see the lights?" he said plainly. Not waiting for an answer, he walked away swiftly. Without hesitation I followed. It was an invitation from a brother that never acknowledged my existence.

I knew that if a living soul were outside, he wouldn't risk being seen with his only sister. Still I was pleased.

Jerry didn't notice that I had trouble keeping up.

Unencumbered by books as I was, he took long strides, absorbed in the decorations. Nothing was too insignificant for his scrutiny. This was a brother that I did not know. This was a first unabashed ardor he had in something. Here was an intensity I never imagined he owned.

Hoping he was taking only that one side street, I knew I would not have chosen this path. I was already freezing with the wind whipping around my exposed lean limbs. I, too, admired the Christmas lights, but I didn't love them enough to endure such pain. When it was unbearable I walked backwards. Jerry would never do such a thing.

In the dark, I notice that Jerry was shivering. He wore neither hat, nor gloves. Though I thought he was nuts, I wondered who was crazier - Jerry for loving the lights, or me, for desiring his company.

By the second side street it was clear that he had no plans to head home until he has seen everything in the valley. I agonized. But then, I continued with him, still thinking about my fellow Girl Scout friends warm and safe at home by that time. The straps on my book bag were digging into my shoulders. I was sure the books weighed more than I did. We walked silently. At times, Jerry would stop at certain displays. I would catch up and have time to stand on one leg to warm the other under my coat and uniform jumper.

Though he made sounds of appreciation for certain decorations, Jerry didn't communicate with me. I knew better than to speak to this boy who felt no compulsion to respond. Never did I complain that I was hungry that I was exhausted, that my bladder was full, or that, did I mention, I was COLD. The pins and needles tingling in my legs had stopped. They were numb. Theoretically I could have headed home any time. Yet I did not. At each juncture I stayed loyal to this course of action. I could take it. I was tough. Still, I prayed that he would take a short cut.

As we rounded the last street and approached our own, we both knew we missed supper. We knew that we would be in trouble. There was no need to mention it. It was inevitable. We were willing to pay the consequences.

Our parents were justifiably upset, angry and irate. Jerry simply walked coolly past all the uproar and disappeared into his room. He was immune and impervious to the drama, as if nothing was happening. God, how I wished I could be like him. He could walk past any scene as if it was a TV set and turn it off.

Strangely, my parents cornered me, never noticing that Jerry was involved. His door was shut, leaving me alone in the center of the storm. Stopped in my tracks both physically and emotionally, I could not move. Dad, who ordinarily was slow to anger, was already boiling over at my terrible thoughtlessness. Didn't I know they would worry? Mother, screaming, yelling and crying, went from hysterics to fearfulness seeing on my face red blotches, a sign of superficial frostbite.

It took hours of stinging pain getting normal circulation back in my face, hands and legs. It took hours before the pain left my skin. It took days before my parents stopped seething at my poor judgment.

None of that mattered very much to me. It was, after

all, worth it. I had entered my brother's world and it was fascinating. I glimpsed a side of him that I have never forgotten. I spent privileged time that was rare indeed. Here was an interest, a passion closely hidden in an impenetrable brother, who seemed, until then, oblivious of everyone and everything.

To this day, I love Christmas lights. I love to canvas the whole neighborhood for decorations. Now I do it by car.

A LIVING PINCUSHION

"Come here," my mother would beckon me with the box of pins in her hand. Knowing what that meant, I wanted to run. Since my emaciated frame disallowed a normal fit unless it was altered, I had to stand still so my mother could hem my clothes. Since almost everything I owned was a hand-me-down, I was used to clothes not fitting, but some clothes were literally touched the ground when I tried them on. Most clothes I received were impractical for use, unless hemmed and pulled in at the waist.

While I thought I had my own clothes when I was a young child, by elementary school I knew that my clothes were all second-hand. Some were from my twin cousins who were seven years older than I was. Other clothes came from the thrift store. Some were found in the trash. All of it was long out of style. To make matters worse, I was short and scrawny, therefore hard to fit.

"Stand up straight," my mother commanded with the force of a major sergeant. "She's doing me a favor," I told myself. Though I knew I should be grateful, I was merely submissive.

Standing up straight was a concept that I couldn't wrap my mind around. Unable to breathe, I had the posture of a strange rag doll with stooped shoulders. My legs were wobbly from the sure knowledge that those legs would be hit at any moment for no apparent reason.

When my mother wanted me to turn, she never said: "Turn." She just stung my legs with the side of her measuring stick and pointed. Other times she hit my legs because I was not still enough. It was slow torture. It took an agonizing eternity for one hem. She would stare at my skinny self, sizing me up. It was a blank stare that was creepy.

Whenever I was stuck with a pin, she accused me of not standing straight enough to avoid her 'accidents.' Feeling like a pincushion, I was told I was to blame. Unable to look down for fear of not standing straight, I did not understand why it took so long.

I implored her to let me measure the clothes with a similar clothes item that fit. She would only hit my legs harder. The physical pain was merely uncomfortable. The tension was far more objectionable. The way she looked at me worse. Not knowing when I would be hit and the harsh tone of voice were the worst parts of the ordeal. Still, I yearned to turn into the good statue that she wanted me to be.

To her credit, Mother taught me to sew on her sewing machine. To this day, I am grateful. By age 10, I learned to sew well enough to hem clothes by hand or machine myself, so I resisted her attempts to measure clothes on me. Using my uniform as a measure I realized that all one needs to do is mark a hem with one pin initially, then measure the rest of the hem on that one. All that standing was unnecessary.

Most of the time, Mother never finished sewing my hems. Often, she ended up giving away the second-hand clothes that she forced me stand up for. Throughout high school years, I had one uniform jumper dress and two uniform blouses. For after school, I sewed some skirts, but never found blouses to go with them. I had one dress I bought with my babysitting money, one skirt and one blouse that my mother found, all in need of hems. So, I sewed the little I had, and this pincushion was free.

SECRETS

Colleen was the new fourth grade student. In the middle of the day and in the middle of the school year, the principal brought her in. Standing there, Colleen's big smile warmed me. Immediately I wished I could be Colleen, even though I wouldn't want to be standing alone in the front of the room. Not having a uniform yet, she was wearing cute clothes. She was the prettiest girl in this class of 52 students.

At lunchtime I checked on her. No one was talking to her. Maybe they thought she liked being by herself since she seemed very confident alone. When I spoke with her, I noticed that she was not all that interested in me, despite wanting me around. Colleen knew what she wanted and went after it. She was the star and I was the audience.

That day Colleen got on my school bus. She got off about a quarter mile before my bus stop. Each day we rode together back and forth. We'd see each other in the same classroom and play on the same schoolyard. I invited Colleen to do things at school. She did not seem to warm up to me, or to anyone. Since I already had lots of friends, especially Barb, Danielle, Jane, and Sandy, I didn't mind.

My mother met Colleen's mother at church. Mother claimed that she liked Colleen because her parents were from Ireland, like Mother's and Dad's parents. I didn't think that was the only reason. Mother told me daily: "Why don't you go over to Colleen's and play?"

I'd feign deafness to the command wrapped in a question.

One day in fifth grade, Colleen came to my house. Catching Jerry in the living room. It was a rare time he was outside his bedroom-hiding place. Colleen focused on him, not even pretending to be visiting me. While she sat by him on the sofa where he stretched out, Jerry pushed her on the floor and moved back to his room.

Hearing Jerry's commotion, Mother came in. Colleen suggested that she wanted **me** to go out for a walk. It was sub-zero weather. Since ice-covered snow had been on the ground for weeks and since cold air made it hard to breathe, I gave a firm NO. "Too much homework," I protested.

Colleen, of course, said she wasn't doing it, so I didn't need to do it either. I asserted that I had to study harder to keep up with her. Mother insisted loudly that I go out. In her opinion, I needed fresh air all of a sudden. Saying "no" to Mother made her more insistent. Colleen didn't mind my emotional discomfort, my obvious unwillingness, or my explanation of physical distress on such a bitter cold day. She waited patiently until I gave in to Mother's demands.

That time, and every time, I went out with Colleen, I got into some difficulty. That day, she wanted me to walk over a huge snowdrift that covered a dirt pile. Pulling me along she assured me she had gone over it earlier and it was safe. Colleen had the persistence trait like my mother had. Sinking in, my boot came off and filled up with snow and mud. It was an especially long, cold unpleasant walk home freezing my foot while carrying one wet, mud soaked boot that splattered all over my coat.

Another time, at an outdoor ice-skating pond, Colleen led me to thin ice that would not have held me had I listened to her. Making a practice out of goading people into doing risky things, was normal for her. When she couldn't get me to do it, she manipulated someone else into falling into thin ice that cold day. Just seeing that was upsetting for me. Silently I left without a as much as a goodbye.

Another time, while showing me a private, densely wooded area, she ditched me, leaving me alone to find my way out. With determination, I swore I'd never hang out with her again.

As we entered high school, I noticed that she was less mischievous and more serious and unhappy. Fear and insecurity traveled as her most constant cohorts. I suspected they were her only companions. On several occasions she sought me out as she rambled half-bragging about her latest abusive, handsome boyfriend.

Once, as I was walking home from visiting Barb, Colleen saw me and walked beside me. No longer that pretty girl I first saw in fourth grade, she was scared and coarse looking. Her desire to be with me was not flattering. I was still the audience.

Already I had heard the rumors that her drunken father beat her up on a regular basis. Hoping that it was not true, I was silent on the matter and so was she.

Colleen did tell me that she was worried about her

grades. "Why?" I blurted out. "You are so smart!"

"I know the stuff; I just can't put it on the test page," she explained. Never having heard of that, I figured that it could very well be true, especially if her father was such a disturbance in her life.

Long after high school, when her father was incarcerated for drinking, I discovered that it was true. Then, people close to the family reported seeing bruises on Colleen.

Despite the fact that it was not her fault, I know Colleen felt shame. Understanding her reluctance to speak of it, I could relate. Not knowing what to say to make it better, I did not reach out.

Though most people knew about my mother, I was silent on my own secret agony. Others kept the secret they knew about me. It was the world we inhabited. Knowing that I could not speak to Colleen about her life, I understood why others could not share what they knew about my life. Since none of us ever spoke the obvious, we all were complicit in the belief that some things were too awful to mention. What could not be said, spoke volumes. It is also what kept us locked in our prison of self-judgments and shame.

WHAT IS ACCEPTABLE?

While still in grade school, I observed my Mother on warm nights, sleeping on the grass in the front yard. Actually the back yard was bigger, but it did not suit my mother's purposes. The front yard was definitely more public and Mother had a propensity for drama. It was "too hot inside," she explained succinctly.

Wearing her ragged bedclothes, she usually came in after the men on the street drove passed on their way to work. That included Dad who would see her there.

One morning, after a week of those grass-sleeping nights, men in white coats came to the house. Dad hadn't left for work yet. At the door, the men spoke to him privately for a moment. Then I heard them asked where to find her. Dad pointed to the bedroom where Mother had just come inside to rummage around for God-knows-what. The screaming started as the two men took her by the arms. She didn't fight them physically as I knew she could. Like a scared rabbit, she was just yelling from the surprise of the ambush.

Dad observed the scene as a bystander. It was likely a surprise to him, but his demeanor never gave it away. When she was out of sight and hearing, I asked Dad if it was due to the sleeping in the grass that led to this. "No, it was the noise and digging into neighbors' garbage cans that did it," he answered flatly as if nothing just happened. I got ready for school as always, and tried not to think of where she was going. My brothers had no reaction.

Walking to the bus stop, I lost myself in pondering what was the dividing line between sanity and insanity. "What behavior constituted normal and what constituted the unacceptable?" Making noise, digging in trashcans, and even displaying herself on the lawn didn't seem that bad to me, especially compared to her anger flares, sudden nastiness, chilling screams, etc. I guess it had to do with *who* was disturbed. The relatives and the neighbors knew some of the extremes that went on. They had seen and heard her howling and hitting us. They kept that to themselves. The people who saw her reactions to her children, looked away.

Yet, when odd behavior bothered and affected them, then it wasn't all right anymore. It all seemed a blur to me. What got her put away didn't seem anywhere near as serious as lots of other things that didn't have consequences. I could never have gotten away with the things my mother was permitted to do.

Knowing that Dad didn't call the men in white coats, I was secretly glad to have neighbors that did.

PLEASING DAD

When Dad was at home, Mother would not scream as often as when he was at work. She shouted orders, but not with quite the same cruel sharpness to it. On one particular Saturday, trying to appeal to some sense of fairness, I protested that it was not my turn to do the huge pile of dishes.

Saturdays were sports days. Dad was drinking beer and listening to the game on the radio, while hearing the commotion Mother made about my protests. "Do what you're told," he predictably said, not knowing all that I had done already. Mother looked pleased, knowing that my objections would have continued if Dad weren't home.

As I had done many times, I had scrubbed the stove that was grubby and disgusting. The grime was deep and thick and did not come off with the dishrag that I was handed. Rubbing with dish soap and water, I toiled away while feeling defeated by the stove and by Mother. No cleaning exercise ever came out well. Mother said she was teaching me the responsibilities that I would have on my own. My feeling was that it couldn't happen soon enough, though I was only eleven.

After lots of frustrating work with minimal results, I realized that Mother never cared about anything actually getting clean. She just wanted me to work.

When the baseball game was over, Dad announced that he was going to get groceries. I saw my opportunity and offered to go help Dad. He agreed to have my company, despite not needing help.

Before getting the groceries, Dad stopped at a bar that he frequented. Jokingly, he said he would let me put my feet up in the bar counter, but that he would not let me drink anything. When I got inside the murky, smoke filled place, I disliked the dark, dingy room. Dad seemed to relish it. I thought he did not belong in that environment. The men did not look like professionals.

Dad got a beer with a chaser. Detesting the smell of the liquor and the smoke, I could not imagine what he saw in the all-male enclave. Somehow he thought I'd be honored to be there, but I was only impressed with the honor of his company, while being dismayed by the bar company he chose.

After the boring shopping and the stop at the bar, my father told me at home that I needed to learn how to drink. Pouring a shot of rye, he told me that it would "put hair on my chest." With my round back and my inverted chest, I looked like the letter C with legs.

Figuring that hair didn't belong on my chest, I worried that I might not get anything else growing there. Swallowing the liquor in two gulps, I pretended it tasted all right while my mouth and throat were on fire. My father was proud, as if it was the best thing that I ever did.

This drinking accomplishment seemed to make him happier than my ability to discuss the player performance of all the professional baseball teams. At dinner every night for the previous two years, I had learned the facts of all the baseball players and the scores of all the teams in both leagues. I knew which team was in which place and which teams were likely to go to the playoffs. Buying and trading baseball cards, I knew every Philadelphia Phillies player and his batting average so that I would have a lot to say at dinnertime. I knew which team was in which place and which teams were likely to go to the playoffs. It was my father's favorite topic in the spring and summer. I had no interest other than impressing my dad.

So Dad and I had a drinking ritual that we did from time to time. "Since I could do this," I supposed, "maybe I would turn out to be O.K. after all. One needs to be good at something."

MONEY

Having been teens at the start of the Great Depression, my parents lived with extreme frugality. One example was that Christmas was often delayed so that my parents could shop for bargains after Christmas. After the Santa myth was dispelled, we received nothing on Christmas Day except the promise of 'After Christmas' sales. The bargains afterwards weren't what we wanted, but that was no deterrent to my parents.

Nothing was bought unless it was urgent like bills or food. Food was bought below full price whenever possible. Mostly everything else was considered frivolous. "Waste not, want not" was the family theme. Actually, it was more like: "Spending is a sin, unless you'll literally die without spending on what's needed."

One day my parents decided to burn the trash in an outdoor fireplace. Dad, of course, led the project that took hours for him and Mother. They gathered paper items from all the rooms. It was amazing for Mother to let go of anything, so this was quite the sight to see. From inside, I watched the fire.

Later that day, Dad asked where were the two one hundred dollar bills that he had brought home from the bank that day. Mother answered that it was sitting on the arm of the sofa, but now it was gone. They searched the house in great frenzy. The only conclusion was that the money slipped into the trash can next to the sofa. The realization that my parents, who would cling to a penny, had actually burned $200 was a shock. That was equivalent to two months salary for Dad at that time. While feeling their pain, their fear and their guilt, I wondered momentarily if Mother would be more careful where she put important things from then on. It wasn't long when I knew nothing would ever change.

SIBLING BONDING...OVER A FREEZER

With the family mantra focused on financial savings, we children were amazed at first that Dad bought a freezer one day when I was twelve. To make room for it, he diligently removed all the debris from a corner of the den. The freezer was huge, gleaming white with silver clamps. It opened by lifting the lid from the top. Kept in the den, it brought shiny hope to my heart.

For Dad, this was a money-saving device. He could buy 'day old' bread and store it. On the money he saved, the freezer would pay for itself, he reasoned. The bread he bought was actually far older than a day out-of-date for regular sales, but "day old" was the label the store used. He wanted to believe the store.

Nutritional value meant nothing. We kids were so hungry that we often ate the bread frozen. Everything in the kitchen refrigerator was moldy, curdled, or disgusting in some way. Eventually, Dad splurged on 'day old' cupcakes. There were two cupcakes in a pack. Some were vanilla cupcakes with cream inside and some packs were strawberry cakes with pink marshmallow icing. My favorite was the third choice: chocolate icing with cream inside. For sure, too hungry to wait for defrosting, we ate cupcakes frozen, also.

At first, we shrewdly left a few cupcakes so Dad would have some for his lunch through the week. Eventually, these considerations dissolved into leaving one last cupcake pack. No one wanted to eat the last cupcake. Finally, probably within a month, there was little or nothing left for Dad.

Mother never caught us eating from the trough like the little desperate domestic animals we were. Usually, we'd make our raids when she was napping. That gave us a lot of latitude. When awake and out of sight, she was busy messing up the disorder of the house even further. Also, when Mother was yelling at one of us, the other two of us would use that time to make a run to the freezer.

However, many times the three of us would meet by the freezer not by design, but by frustration with the food supply. There were things in the refrigerator, but nothing that was edible.

Then Dad began to buy cheap ice cream to store in this treasure chest. What a bonanza! The three little pigs would meet at the freezer with whatever silverware or tool we could find to pry the ice cream out. Eating directly from the box, we were unconcerned about germs. They were the least of our worries.

Never did we discuss our emotional pain when we were together there, though that freezer was the only meeting place we had alone. It was the closest thing to intimacy we had together.

Enjoying those moments, we were gleeful and elated whenever we had time to dig in whether alone, or with each other. It was more fun and less guilt when we were together. We delighted in the collective bond of hunger, and thievery. There was also the risk factor of getting caught. It was unsafe to go there, since

Mother might find us and it would not go well. Dad would not have approved either.

Still, Dad was not obtuse about the low frozen supplies left each week. He may have thought that Mother was eating a lot. So he just bought more without complaining.

With all we stole, I'm sure that Dad never saved any money with the freezer. He just might have saved our lives though, despite the fact that the frozen food had no nutritional value.

SOUNDS

Mother liked the sound of her voice. Incessantly, she talked to anyone who even seemed like they were listening, whether in person, or on the phone. Frequently, I was the chosen audience. Before I left home at 17, it was in person. As an adult I was the audience over the phone. Repeatedly, she told me nonstop stories of her childhood. She thought she was always the heroine, but from a young age, I knew there was nothing to admire.

Barking orders, she called for any of us to do something. With an endless supply of commands, she never tired of being the boss.

Actually Mother bellowed relentlessly when she was not telling stories about herself. In the car, she read every passing sign as if every one of them was important. That was unlike her children who were clearly not important and whose names she could never remember.

And when she slept... yes, she snored loudly, too. Much later in life, she made constant clicking sounds with her tongue throughout the day. To my knowledge, no one ever asked her to stop.

MOTHER'S SELF-EXPRESSION

Weekends were Dad's days to unwind with his beloved radio ball game and copious amounts of beer with chasers. He smoked a lot, too. The kitchen became his station as he stood near the radio, probably so no one else had to hear it any louder than it was. The real reason may have been that he knew that Mother would not be there in the kitchen.

On one particular day when I was ten years old, Dad bought paint for the kitchen at Mother's insistence. Not just one color. Mother wanted both pink and white.

Everyone knew Dad did not like to paint. Besides, pink was not his color, for sure. It is not that he had a color. If he did, it would likely have been gray. I admired Dad for doing that labor of love without complaint.

With breathing problems, I felt like I would suffocate with the smell of paint. I wondered how I would ever survive later in life if I had to paint a room. It was midsummer and the heat was agonizing, long before noon. The sweltering was more than I could take. It was too scorching to go outside. With the smell of paint through the main part of the house, I had more trouble than ever breathing.

It took Dad all day. Dutifully, he painted the opposite walls the same color. Two pink and two white walls made it hard to get the corners straight, so that paint didn't leak into the adjacent wall. Dad even painted the drawers pink and the cabinets white, just as Mother directed. By nightfall, he put away the paint cans, brushes and ladder.

The verdict came in. Yes, it was different. And yes, surprisingly it looked crisp and clean, especially compared to the dirty green previously on the walls. We were impressed. We had never seen a two-color combo. This was one crazy idea of Mother's that wasn't all bad. Quietly, I told Dad that I liked what he did.

As darkness was falling, I went to bed early just to get as far away from the kitchen paint smell. Staying up to watch TV was always risky anyway, since Mother had a habit of turning it off when it got interesting.

With no viable alternatives, I went through the door to the bedroom area. Closing the door to my room off the hall, I tried to breathe though the outside air was still muggy. There was no escape and no relief.

Most nights I sat up all night wishing I could die and just get it all over with. Sitting up as usual, I pondered if this really was my last breath since it was such a struggle both inhaling and exhaling. Amazingly, the struggle just continued as I watched the minutes go by and I accepted the end of it all. Remembering the extremely cold nights were just as hard to take as the extremely hot ones, I watched the evening light gradually switch to sundown. Eventually the need for sleep overruled the need to breathe.

In the morning, I was mystified how I made it through the night. I always awoke sleep deprived and usually shocked into consciousness. Rudely awakened by the sound of loud radio music, my father thought that was a clever way to wake us up. One of us, he explained, was slow to get up, so all of us had to hear this monstrous sound much louder than was necessary to rouse hibernating bears.

We had thirty minutes to get dressed and eat before leaving the house for Sunday Mass. Soon we met in the newly painted kitchen to get ourselves some stale cereal and rancid skim milk.

Mother was there already. Immediately, I noticed the painted cabinets and drawers. There were words written in crayon, pencil and pen. Seeing it, I felt deeply disappointed. I stopped and looked around. The nice kitchen couldn't last. I knew it. But so soon? I was not prepared. I regretted going to bed early and not enjoying the kitchen while it was new. My face clearly told the story.

Mother glared ready to pounce on me, as if I was the one who had defaced the room. She wanted me to say something, so she could defend herself. Giving me away, my face had already said enough.

Silently, first searching for milk in a mold-infested refrigerator, I hunted for cereal, bowl and spoon. Wherever they were, it was not where a normal person would expect. While one spoon was in a drawer, it was clearly unwashed. I decided to use it anyway since washing it was a problem. The dishrag was filthy. The sink, full of caked-on dirty dishes, smelled.

Finding a bowl was another matter. A bowl could be any room except the kitchen. Bowls would be wherever Mother had a whim to put them. Knowing how cunning and creative she was, I wasn't in the mood. So I took the dirty bowl left on the table. Probably Dad used it because I heard him leaving the kitchen earlier. I sat down silently with my dissatisfaction. Seven-year-old brother Eddie came in. "What's this?" was his instant, innocent inquiry about the cabinets.

"What! Don't you like it?" Mother shrieked. "This way I'll know where to find things" she justified.

I wiggled in my seat with this piece of news. "Wow, when did she ever want to know where anything was?" I questioned silently. She had far too much fun playing the 'lost' game.

I dared not look up, much less say how ridiculous that was, as I kept looking at the anemic and curdled milk in the bowl. I knew Mother added water to the skim milk to save money. No one wanted to drink much milk, so it went bad before it was used up. That might have been the purpose.

Twelve-year-old Jerry came in. As usual, he searched for a bowl, gave up, and asked me when I'd be finished with mine. He showed not the slightest reaction to the kitchen 'décor.'

Not a thing surprised him, or he had a good pretense reflex. He appeared to not notice and not care. I marveled at his demeanor. For him, nothing happened before Dad's painting or after Mother's graffiti. Either nothing mattered to him, or he was smarter than Eddie and me.

THE VBT

Mother had two kinds of times. She had bad times. And she had Very Bad Times (VBT). Thankfully, the bad times were the majority of days.

During the VBT, Mother was more agitated than usual and more likely to go into rage. The house reflected her mood, which was never subtle.

The bedroom my parents shared was already dangerous to navigate on a regular day. Mother's clothes littered the floor and you could not see the rug.

Their small bedroom wallpaper I despised. It depicted large, dark, maroon-colored, decaying roses. The bureau top held numerous miscellaneous items all covered with white talcum powder mixed with equal parts gray dust.

Mother prized body powder. Like everything else, the powder was not accessible. Rather, it was spilled all over the bureau top rendering it useless. The powder puff was exposed, tattered and sullied over years of neglect. Mother had added a box of baking soda to the cheap body powder and most of the mix overflowed what was once an empty powder box. Peculiar, unusable things were mixed in with the dirty powder on the bureau surrounded the box. There had been a hand mirror on the bureau and it was not clear enough to see any reflection.

The bedroom closet was full of clothes that did not fit and required repairs. Everyone else's clothes were problematic in their closets too, though no closet had the number of clothes that my parents had. It wasn't that they bought a lot, it was that Mother "found" things and could never let anything go.

If I could help it, I did not go in to my parents' bedroom. When I was summoned, I felt guilty walking on things, but moving things took too long and no one could hold in their hands all the obstacles in the way.

The dysfunction did not stop at the bedroom. To bathe in the tub, each of us had to move the three feet by five feet clutter-tub of about a hundred ever-changing items, most of which were utterly worthless.

Occasionally I fantasized about saving time.

I could dig into the center of the bathtub pile and make just enough room for my feet. But I knew the items would move and slide. Even if I could have managed it, they would have caved in on my skinny legs. Though the thought was tempting to try, I knew I couldn't get away with it. There would always be more hell to pay, as if I didn't have my fill already.

Always there was a box of socks with holes. I had to help Mother darn the socks whenever I wanted to read. No matter how many I sewed and she sewed, the box just got bigger. Often I suspected that she found them that way in someone's trash. Some didn't have mates, so I quietly put those at the bottom of the box. Mother chastised my choices, insisting that wearing mixed-matched socks was not a problem. In a way, she had a point. What was matched today, would be lost tomorrow. Then we would be back to mixed-matched.

Whenever I was going somewhere, I was required to take socks, thread, and needle with me. I was too stubborn to darn anything, but I'd refer to her in my head as "Darn Mother" when I went out with the sewing supplies pretending I would follow orders. Being required to take it with me, did not mean anyone could make me actually darn them.

At a young age, I learned that life was difficult and unruly. Frustration ruled. Simple maintenance was fraught with obstacles since daily infrastructure was turbulent and the foundation was unstable.

Disturbance governed each day with a brutal streak. It lived intimately within every part of my life, my body, and my environment.

Those were the regular times.

In the Very Bad Times, the typical chaos was not extreme enough for Mother. Her choices of ragged clothes got even more exaggerated.

Mother would overturn chairs. This way she could "fix them from underneath." Even after Dad allowed several weeks of this, nothing could convince Mother that it was time to turn the chairs upright. It had to happen in her time, on her schedule. From the start, even she knew she had no intention of fixing anything.

Another sign of her VBT was that she was not satisfied with disordered drawers. Contents of jammed drawers morphed into disarrayed floors as she dumped and overturned them. So she could "straighten them out," Mother emptied out everything. The drawer contents were strewn everywhere possible on floors and on already fully cluttered tables. On these VBT, it meant that we had to watch where we walked throughout the house.

It was amazing how much litter could be emptied out of even one drawer. There were two drawers that fit under the coffee table, two deep drawers on the end tables and four drawers on a desk. That desk was constantly covered with trash rendering it impossible to use in regular times.

Mother would accept no offer to help her sort things. You might lose some of her valuables, she reasoned. From that rubble on floors, you could break your neck falling on some slick advertisement from six years ago. You could step on broken pencils, rusty scissors, non-functioning watches, mysterious nails, scrunched scrap paper, dead leaves, random string, stretched rubber bands, loose powder, unusable keys, and crushed paper bags with remnants of sandwiches. All were in zigzag layers piled on top of one another. The dispersed contents were a bizarre and curious mix.

That was just the small clutter. The large drawers held massive things that were scattered about the house, never to be put away again. I was grateful that the sofa was too heavy for her to move. Otherwise, we would not have had anywhere to sit down during those weeks. Yet, the cushions disappeared since they 'needed mending.' So we sat on the sofa springs amidst the debris caught in the springs. Though uncomfortable, fortunately the sofa had covered springs, unlike the bedsprings that were open and exposed to accumulations of inches of visible dust particles.

Luckily Mother didn't take the mattresses off the beds. There really was nowhere to store those anywhere else. Besides, Mother was IN bed too much for her to take the mattress away. That would be inconvenient for her.

Discarding anything was not permitted. She would cry, scream, and hit the offender. Though none of the stuff was worth saving, it seemed to me that she valued these things more than she valued any of us. She would protect her stuff with all her life. Things appeared more important to her than people. Even when it came to people, Mother apparently believed that anyone else was more valuable than her family.

Pandora's opened box was no stranger in our house. Chaos controlled every inch of space virtually all the time. At these VBTs, Pandora's Box opened up and attacked the house with the vengeful force of hurricane proportion. The drawers were freed, and we were held hostage.

These VB Times occurred at least two to three times a year. Dad was infinitely long-suffering and hardly noticed the difference. He never complained about the clutter and the dirt. I figured that he did not mind.

Yet later, his patience was not as great when it came to me. Often when I washed my stockings in the bathroom sink, Dad wouldn't wait three minutes for the cold wash liquid to take effect on the stockings I had to wear each day as part of my uniform. He would wash his hands or rinse toothpaste out of his mouth all over my stockings. I suppose the bathroom sink was his last straw. After all, the only other sink was in the kitchen, full of dishes.

Hair

One thing I knew for sure growing up was that my straight hair was unacceptable. The night before I had somewhere to go, my straight hair was rolled up in rags so tight it hurt my scalp. Even when all the rags stayed in, I looked like an unnatural, messy mishmash throughout the day.

Yet often during the night, I'd pull some rags off, while only partially aware of the ramifications in the morning. That was most of the time. The results made me look beyond ridiculous.

My stubbornness ruled when my mother insisted that if I ate carrots daily, my hair would curl. I didn't care enough. So it was my fault my hair was an embarrassment to my mother.

The solution for other straight haired girls was to have Toni perms. Thankfully, my mother didn't do that. It cost money so that was out. Same with hair spray. Neither would not have been healthy for me. I'm OK with the fact that money was the issue, not health.

Never was I enrolled in what was socially subscribed. Really, I had a whole lot more pressing and immediate concerns than how screwy my hair looked.

As a teenager paying for my own haircuts, all the hairdressers wanted to do was curl my hair and spray it heavily. It never worked. My hair fell back to its original straight before I made it out of the salon.

Finally, I boldly told a hairdresser who was new to me, that I wanted my hair cut so it looked nice straight. He replied that if I didn't want it curled, he'd give me a bag to wear over my head.

Though that hairdresser was more blunt than most, I had to admit it wasn't a common style to have straight hair. So, because he laughed at me, I left without allowing the curls, silently vowing never to return.

My first perm happened in order to celebrate my 40th birthday. It took two tries from that same hairdresser, because the first didn't take. The two tries were my first and last attempts at wavy hair. The curly surprise was so radical for my friends, some literally screamed when they saw me. It was fun to have curly hair, but the smell and the pain didn't seem worth it. Evidently, I'm not terribly attached to looking good.

With the laid-back late 60's, the hippy message was to 'let it be.' Straight hair became socially acceptable in some circles. Now all these years later, it is not an issue. And I still don't care.

LOVE THY NEIGHBOR

Behind our house lived a family I knew well for many years. Two parents, a son Billy, a daughter Nancy, and a newborn Rob occupied the house. The father was drunk most of the time that he was home.

Billy was in my 7th grade class and Nancy was in 6th grade. They played outdoor games with the dozen of us in the neighborhood. When their mother had baby Rob, ostensibly I went over to help her out after school and on days when no neighborhood games were being played. Really, I wanted to get out of the house.

Mrs. Finley really liked my presence and invited me to visit often. As an avid sports viewer, she loved the seasonal teams all year on TV. It was a distraction for her. When I came over, she turned off the TV sports she loved. Often Billy and Nancy were out, presumably looking for somewhere else to go.

At times, I arrived at the door and heard her husband screaming at her. Quickly and quietly, I hurried away not wanting anyone to know I heard.

As a nurse, Mrs. Finley worked on weekends and nights while her husband was home with the children. Gradually he was home less and less until he stayed somewhere else.

Helping her clean and playing with her baby, I felt accepted and useful. After a few years, Mrs. Finley confided in me that she was getting a divorce. Immediately, I understood the red eyes and the stress

I saw many times. Her eyes blinked more often than anyone's I ever knew. The lone adult in the house for quite awhile, she was resigned to her fate.

Not knowing anyone else who was divorced, I was stunned at her harsh reality. In our Catholic world, divorce was a sin, always wrong for whatever reason. Yet, I couldn't believe that Mrs. Finley was doing something bad. Naturally loving her, I offered her solace.

When it was no longer a secret about the divorce, I spoke to my parents about possibly helping Mrs. Finley. It was surprising that my parents did not hold the idea of divorce against her. They told me that her husband beat her, was unfaithful, and spent her earnings. Since Mrs. Finley was very private, it was amazing to me how much personal information was public knowledge in that small suburb.

When school was out the next summer, Mrs. Finley sold her house and left her three children to her sister's care in a neighboring state. Waiting for her divorce to come through, she needed a place to stay. In an act of unusual generosity and open-mindedness, my parents took her in for a few months.

While Mrs. Finley worked two hospital shifts, she'd come to our house late at night and sleep with me in my single bed. Observing how thoroughly exhausted she was, I saw how hard life can be for an adult. Not only did she miss her children, she had no partner to rely on.

While neither of us took up a lot of space, sleeping in my twin-size bed with Mrs. Finley made it a very tight squeeze. I loved her being there. Despite all the stress she endured, she cared about me. She took an active role in my health and brought different types of breathing medicine to me from the hospital. Though I was conflicted about accepting stolen goods, I was excited to discover that there were medicines that could help. Trouble was, when she moved the medicine stopped, too.

Since I had already started making money by charging for babysitting children of other neighbors, I began buying over-the-counter respiratory products. They were rescue medicines to be used during breathing difficulty, which was most of the time. There was nothing I knew to use for prevention. The family doctor didn't offer anything outside of an injection of Epinephrine when my parents thought I might die. Still, I was in dire need most of the time. So Mrs. Finley brought new medicines that educated me to what was available.

Yet, more than physical help, this nurse-angel brought some emotional support. Besides nurturing me, she listened. As if I mattered, she asked me questions and wanted my opinion.

When she was ready to leave, I was happy for her new life reunited with her children. And, I was brokenhearted. Though I cared about her children that I interacted with for years, I had loved their mother more. She had given me respect, and I adored her.

We kept in touch for a while. Then she vanished when she moved a second time.

Later, the word got around that in another city her ex-husband Mr. Finley died from his long alcoholism. None of the neighbors, or their children, regretted the loss. No one much cared.

Jack, a friend of Billy's, said that the world was better off. For me, it felt sad and unjust, for the three children who had little time, if any, with a sober father.

SUMMER WEEKDAYS

It happened everyday I lived at home. Looking right at me as though the house mess was all my doing, Mother pointed to the dirty dishes in the sink and addressed me as "Eddie," then quickly said: "No, Jerry." At last in frustration she shouted: "Eleanor," her sister's name. Looking like a bulldog, she got angrier; as if it is my fault she couldn't remember my name. Mother rarely got my name right. When she did, it was after everybody else in her world.

While Mother showed kindness by occasionally making a dinner that was edible, and at least once she straightened up my bed, it was even more rare that she spoke without contempt. Mostly she sneered at me like I was a wicked sinner condemned to paying off my sentence.

With all my heart I wanted to disappear. I figured I didn't matter anyway. Mother didn't care who slaved for her. She just wanted to catch any of us and make us do what she refused to do. As soon as I followed her orders, she'd find something else. Mother could not stand to see me resting, or appearing to enjoy myself for a minute.

There was always enough to do, all right. Nothing ever stayed clean for a minute before it got messed up again. Estimating an hour of work washing pots and pans from the last Sundays' omelet and bacon that Dad made, and all the dishes and silverware from the week, I had a sinking feeling. So I told her that I did the dishes the last time. Since she named Eddie first, she must have meant for him, I reasoned out loud. Mother wouldn't budge. She went for the nearest easy target. I happened to be the unfortunate one who let hunger get the better of her judgment.

Like shunning poison ivy, Jerry managed to stay out of the fray by not leaving his bedroom. He may have taken food to his room early in the day. I did not know his strategy. He seemed the least called upon.

Eddie got away with a great deal, too. He had some things going for him. He was male, he was cute, and he was the youngest. "Maybe she was saving him to use later," I once considered, but discarded that thought. Even so, sometimes he got caught in her snares, as well.

Before I could get done, Mother found six other odious things that she wanted me to do. I could not get it all done at the speed she wanted. Her dominant emotion was anger, so she frequently grabbed me by the arm or the hair and pushed me where she wanted me.

Figuring that I had so much invested that day in pleasing her, I assumed that if I just worked harder and longer, maybe she would be happy. So I kept working as fast as I could. Still her voice was filled with contempt.

Not knowing what I did to get this hatred, I assumed she was right in her attitude. Disrespect littered the walls, attached to the floors, draped itself over the furniture and permeated every inch of the house. Distain was her tone and actions.

Though it wasn't part of his nature, that attitude affected my father. Fearing being the object of

Mother's temper, he frequently dished it to us, too.

Working quickly, it became abundantly clear that no amount of work was enough. Continually mad about what was left to do, she shouted, then shook me. With tears welling up and feeling my face flush red hot from anger and defeat, I sat on a chair away from her, near the door keeping her in sight, so I had a lead if I had to escape quickly. I contemplated what I could do to run away.

Just then, in a rage, Mother grabbed my face and banged my head against the window behind me. As soon as she was satisfied with that, I got away to my room. Even that was dangerous since she could and did often break in. Dad never put that lock on my door that I requested frequently. This scenario was not the first time, or the last.

When Dad came home, Mother told him what I did not get done and nothing of what I did accomplish. Refusing to come out for dinner, I went to sleep that night hearing Mother tell Dad all the trouble she had with me that day. Nothing was new. This happened regularly. She would go on and on. It was the last thing that my father heard each night before he went to sleep. Sleeping in the room next to their bedroom, it was also the last thing I heard before I got to sleep. It rolled around in my head while I sat up trying to breathe.

For much of my life, whenever people were uncooperative or unkind, I was sure it was because I wasn't doing something right. Constantly, I had some version of self-blame, such as: "I am a bother to people. I shouldn't be who I am. I should be some other way – the right way."

WHEN THE SUN BROKE THROUGH

For a few years, there was a New Year's tradition. For those years when I was between 9 and 13, my parents took us to the movies on the first day of the year. It was a good plan since Dad didn't have to work and we didn't have school.

The closest movie theater had one movie shown for a few days at a time. One year it was a comedy on New Year's. Sitting next to my Dad, I watched him in adoration. Though stern-faced, he was rarely harsh, at least compared to Mother. "His job must be very serious," I thought. Also, I decided that it must be tough to be the head of such a frenzied household as ours.

At one point during the show, I saw Dad smile. It was then that I realized that I had not seen him grin in... well, I could not remember when. I kept looking at him in amazement. It seemed like the first time I saw him genuinely smile. While he didn't laugh like some others around us, he looked so free and so relaxed. That made me happy.

Often after that, I reminded myself that this smile was there somewhere in him. That comedy induced smile wasn't the same as his shy, self-conscious semi-smile he gave in social situations. No, this was indisputable pleasure. It was like the sun came out after a long dark, cloudy time before you knew there was a sun. His smile has stayed with me forever. I still nurture that image as one might caress a gem in a treasure chest.

THE CALM, AND THEN THE STORM

One Saturday afternoon when I was eleven, Mother was out of the house. We were secretly gleeful that Mother was not home. Watching as Eddie flipped the dials of the TV, I discovered an old movie just starting. Dad walked by the living room and got interested, too. Jerry heard the sound and came in to survey the situation. Less interested was I in the movie, as I was in being together.

It was rare that we were even in one room together outside of the kitchen for dinners. The four of us squeezed onto the sofa as our eyes fixed on the screen. It felt safe, even though it was temporary. It occurred to me that if Mother came in and did her usual routine of turning off the TV, then Dad would be inconvenienced. Mother wouldn't dare. Dad wouldn't tolerate an interruption. All was comfortable.

An hour into the show, I heard the sound of Mother outside, singing at a high pitch. The performance continued for quite awhile. I got uneasy. Coming through the door, immediately she went to the TV, standing in front of it. "Get on the floor now and say a prayer" she commanded as she pulled the plug. Three small heads turned just enough to glimpse Dad, but not enough to be obvious. "What would he do? He must be incensed," I thought. I was. I felt my heart beating faster. "What would Dad do to her? Now he could see what she did to us. He couldn't ignore it, or downplay the effects on others."

We didn't have long to wait. Before I could process it, I witnessed my father getting on his knees, folding his hands in prayer. Three of us children followed in fear. "Hail Mary, full of grace..." Mother led in dead earnest. As the praying was persisting, I was wondering what happened in the movie. "Did the ship captain find the beautiful girl stowaway on board? Did the boat's leak sink the ship with everyone on board? Could the lovers swim? How far was landfall?"

"And lead us not into temptation..." Mother continued. "Oh my God, we were on a different prayer already. When will this end?" My bony knees were getting rug burn. It was cramped between the sofa and the coffee table where I found myself. Wanting there to be a time out, I knew it wouldn't be anytime soon. My back hurt from trying to kneel straight.

When Mother got enough satisfaction, she insisted it was time to get things done. Each of us was ordered to work. I was assigned to clean the pots and pans, an impossible job with the only tools we had -- a dirty dishrag and a drop of liquid dish detergent.

Grudgingly, I moved into the kitchen knowing that, to Mother, nothing and no one counted in that house. For me, there was no one to count on.

DINNER

Arriving home from a day in fifth grade, my eyes caught something bizarre outside. Horrified, I saw a scrawny, dead chicken hanging from a tree. Hating to look at it, I averted my eyes. Feeling genuine disgust, I could not keep quiet. Verbalizing helped me release some of my repulsion.

"Is this a decoration?" I inquired delicately, hoping not to push my mother into an angry outburst. She ignored my insinuation of abominable taste. Feeling her dark mood, and getting no response, I tried humor. "Oh, are you into voodoo now?" I asked as though I had figured it out. "No," my mother answered finally with annoyance, "this I got from someone who came to the door. It was cheap."

"Well, all you paid for were the bones," I impudently asserted. It's possible that Mother had gotten it out of somebody's trash, but then where would someone else have obtained that intact bird? It died before it developed. On top of that, having been dead for a very long time, it had shriveled up. No one in her right mind would buy it. That's why my mother did.

Wincing at the thought, I imagined some tramp coming to the door. Outside of Girl Scouts selling cookies and an occasional encyclopedia salesman, no vendors came in this suburb selling anything, much less this atrocity. I was tempted not to believe the story except that Mother could not drive, and the evidence was right there in front of my eyes.

"I wonder to whom the vender sold the feathers," I commented as I stole a glance at the withered ugly remains hanging from the tree. Distressed to think of it cooked, I knew that it would show up on the dinner table despite the fact that Mother almost never really cooked.

"Anyway, I see that we're having chicken **skin** for dinner," I said dryly. "No," she responded, "It has to tenderize so it will just hang there for a few days." I made a mental note to avoid looking outside for a few days.

"Maybe, we'll get lucky and the birds will eat it," I thought and I dared not utter. It would not have gone well. At any moment, Mother was ready to pounce physically and verbally.

To my knowledge, no one else voiced an objection to the monstrosity. Why bother? It would get you nowhere.

Yes, after about a week we ate chicken skin soup from that unfortunate animal, which likely died of starvation itself. If meat existed in the soup, I could not find it. I considered becoming a vegetarian; however food was scarce at home, and my choices were extremely limited.

THE ESSAY

In my fifth grade class one day, everyone had to write an essay. Sr. Mary Phillip was very dull ordinarily. So this assignment gave us a more creative expression. At least we did not have to answer obtuse questions from those pitiful, ridiculous excuses for textbooks. Most school texts were no more than a bunch of pages stapled together. "Anyone could have easily put those together," I thought. The information was paltry and the presentation was pathetic. The worst was the geography book that did not have even one map in it. No drawing, no outline, no table of contents, no footnotes and no index. It was mind-numbingly boring.

The questions we were expected to answer were moronic. In the hated geography book for instance, each chapter described one South American country, and not all the South American countries , mind you. The questions asked such things as what is exported from that country. I couldn't figure out why I should care, unless I intended to be an importer. Nothing mattered in that fifth grade. The nun teacher was a practiced sleepwalker with her eyes open. Sadly, our class had her again in sixth grade and eighth grade.

So, the essay could be about anything. I called mine: "The Tempest in the Teapot." It described my living conditions, if you could call it living. Actually, I covered up the real meaning and wrote symbolically. No one, I hoped, really knew to what I was really referring.

Weeks later, a letter arrived about a Book Company accepting my essay as one of fifty selected winners for the latest book of essays. I was among the top fifty out of thousands of fifth graders all over the country. That was amazing news to me.

Then a call came in the evening. Standing on the wobbly couch cushion trying to see myself in the mirror, I was wondering if I would ever get facial pimples like other kids. My father called me to the phone. The kind man on the other end informed me that his company wanted to send me a complimentary copy of the Essay Book with my essay and 49 others' essays.

The only cost would be minimal, a $1.50 for shipping and handling. Though I would have loved seeing my name in print, I hesitated since that was 6 weeks allowance for me. So I asked the man to wait while I talked to my father. Dad said it was a scam. "Don't believe it. They publish everyone's essay just to sell these books. It's not worth it."

Back on the phone with a conflicted and heavy heart, I turned down the offer. The man at the other end was very understanding.

In school, I asked others if they received a letter or got a call regarding their essay. No one had.

Dad was not impressed with my writing then, or later. When I was twenty-three, I took a job as a textbook writer for teachers of the mentally handicapped. In hearing the news, my father informed me flatly that throughout history there never were any good women writers.

GIVING AND RECEIVING

Coming home from fifth grade, the school bus stopped at my usual corner. However, that day I was not getting off. Since there was a regional Girl Scout meeting a mile away, I planned to get off later. It was exciting and daunting to meet many new scouts from a variety of troops in the area. This was a first.

Some friends and my brothers got off at my usual stop. To my amazement, my mother was waiting at the stop. Entering the bus, she explained to the driver that she had something for me. Coming down the bus aisle towards me, she wore one of her usual ill-fitting, rumpled cotton dresses, a reject from a second-hand store. I say reject because she didn't buy second-hand clothes unless the used clothing was on clearance.

Completely confused to see her, everything seemed like something out of a movie. It could not be happening to me that my mother would go out of her way like this. Handing me a crumpled used paper bag, she instructed me to share this with all the girls at the meeting. I could hardly grasp this as she turned and walked off the bus. "How long had she stood there? And why?" I could not imagine what was in the bag. After the bus pulled out of sight, I stopped waving to my mother, who was by then disappearing from my view.

Looking at the remaining people on the bus, I wondered how many knew about her. I searched for any hint that they had an opinion of my mother's disheveled hair and clothes. "Hopefully," I thought, "not everyone knows that this is the local crazy woman." I prayed that these fellow riders wouldn't remember who she was. Thankfully, they appeared indifferent to what took place. So I hurriedly looked in the bag. "God knows what it could be," I thought. What it contained stunned me with awe and gratitude.

The paper bag held a large plastic bag of hard candies. How incredibly thoughtful this was. Searching my mind for a reason, it seemed that maybe Mother wanted me to be accepted by this large group of Girl Scouts from several troops. Since I only knew the dozen Girl Scouts from my own troop, there were far more that were unknown at this meeting. It was a stunning thought.

On arriving I felt like I was in a twilight zone. I had to adjust to the new peers, the new leaders, the new activities, and the new mother I just met minutes ago on the bus.

"Who was she after all?" I didn't know my mother as someone capable of this kindness.

Deciding when to bring out the hard candy was problematic. "Do I interrupt the leaders? Maybe later," I decided. The entire time of the long afternoon my whole focus was on the candy that was conflicting me. Covertly, I kept the brown bag inside my school bag at my feet. I didn't want anyone to see it before I brought it out. Often I would touch it as I visualized distributing it. Somehow I doubted I could do it. When cookies were served, I knew I had reached a critical moment, but I told myself that if I revealed the hidden bounty at that time, people would wonder why I said nothing earlier. I knew I was lying to myself about not finding the right moment. Beginning to think of myself as selfish, I accused me of not wanting to share.

"O.K., O.K.," I realized that I didn't want to share. "But why? It was just candy and I couldn't imagine eating all that myself. Why couldn't I give it away? I earned an allowance, so I could buy more if this was so tasty. That was more reason to open the bag and celebrate my mother's sudden generosity." I couldn't understand it, but I couldn't part with this loot. In shame, I kept the sweet stuff hidden all the way home.

At the house, I concealed the treasure in the back of a drawer. Later, fearing it would be found, I moved it under the bed. No chance my mother would look there.

All through the rest of grade school and high school, I felt pangs of guilt. "What a terrible person I am." Often I thought about my mother at the bus stop. I thought about the candy.

Concerned that the candy would be found after I left for a distant college, I threw away the whole untouched bag. Even then I couldn't understand my past inaction or why I could neither share, nor eat it. Anytime before, mere guilt would not have stopped me from eating candy.

Years later while raising my daughter, it came in a flash. I remembered that along with the guilt there was a certain satisfaction in the physical symbol of my mother's love. Like the different colored candies, there are different facets to everyone. This was a facet I rarely saw in my mother and I needed to hold on to it as a reminder. It was then that I could have some empathy for the child I once was.

GENEROSITY

A new girl moved in behind our house. Word got out that she was in fourth grade, a year behind me. She went to the public school so I did not ever run into her. I caught glimpses of her from a distance. She was very pretty.

Uncertain what I was in for, I went to her front door. A tall stately woman, with a perfect steel gray hairdo and attractive clothes, greeted me. She ushered me in, introducing herself as Mrs. Collins. Fascinated with her high cheekbones, she immediately reminded me of an older version of singer Dina Shore, who to me represented beauty, poise, and nobility.

In answer to my question about the mysterious new girl, the older lady invited me to sit down. Immediately, she quizzed me about who I was, where I lived and what school I attended. On that bright afternoon, the room was dark with only the light of the TV.

While feeling cornered myself, I noticed Mr. Collins in a corner sitting as quiet as a church mouse, drinking his beer and watching soap operas.

Politely, Mrs. Collins informed me that her granddaughter Danielle was doing her homework. Shortly, she would be called to come out.

The house was similar to other houses in the neighborhood, yet I felt as though this was a protected castle for the princess who lived there. Soon my suspicions were confirmed. Everything revolved around Danielle.

Twisting in the overstuffed chair, I anxiously awaited getting back out in the sunlight. Yet, I was enticed by the carrot stick of a meeting with this new girl in the neighborhood. Presently, our neighborhood was populated mostly with boys, except for the snobby girl, Cecilia, who lived two streets up. I didn't see much of her and I did not care. Pam had moved to Maine the year before, so I had lots of boys around me.

While I had been having fun playing baseball, basketball, volleyball and table tennis with the boys, I wanted some relief from the competition. Wanting to participate did not mean wanting to win. It was a game and I gave each one my all, but I felt the triumph was in the playing. While I had to admit I loved it when I got the ball in that basket with my famous underhand throw, or when I pitched a winning baseball game and witnessed tough boys declared out, I did not get upset when I lost. It was enough to have respect. It was fun seeing the boys on the other team hate it when I beat them at anything. The guys on my team never let on that I did a good job, but the act of choosing me was acknowledgment enough. It was a success for me that I could play at all, given my lungs suffered. That was a secondary consideration for me.

Just when I thought I could stay no more, Danielle came out of her room, gorgeously arrayed. All prim and proper, she appeared as a flawless, live model emerging from some magazine page.

She was more of a girl than anyone I ever met. Everyday she proved it.

Danielle's grandmother always greeted me warmly whenever I visited after that. She offered me Pepsi and a cookie. She and Mr. Collins would ask me about school and they would talk about their plans to build an extension on the house. They asked me to show them the latest dances. Then they requested I teach Danielle. These adults considered me a real person.

Danielle and I were well matched... only in opposite arenas. Danielle clearly had looks, money, clothes, and style, the things that would become increasingly valuable in our lives as time went on. Having almost none of that, I had an easy time in school and I had success in sports. Danielle struggled with schoolwork, dancing, and throwing or catching a ball. To me, hers were huge handicaps. To her, I was way out in left field. Neither of us would have traded places.

Each having our separate skills, we willingly learned from each other. Volleyball was the only sport she wanted to learn and she let me teach her. Table tennis held no interest for her, and baseball was too rough for Danielle.

The neighborhood boys refused to play softball. They played only hardball that promised to knock you out when you were hit. I knew all about that. The worse part was that every participant had to get up and pretend to feel no pain.

Danielle would have none of that sport. She had no brothers, so she had no need to find her place. Her world was completely on her terms.

When I taught Danielle volleyball, her grandparents were thrilled. They bought all kinds of equipment for her.

The next year, when I was invited to a big 6th grade party at a schoolmate's home, I despaired since it was a dress-up event. My decision was not to go and not to tell my parents. Danielle was the only one to whom I confided. A few days later, miraculously Mrs. Collins gave me a huge bag filled with a beautiful dressy dress. As I looked at it in astonishment, she explained that Danielle had outgrown it and she wanted me to have it. Not only was Danielle taller and fuller than I was, her bones were bigger and shoulders much wider. It was hard to imagine she ever wore a dress that would fit me. Never had I seen the dress on her, nor had I seen it in her closet of fabulous clothes that showed me often. This formal dress looked new.

Yet the implication that a brand new dress presented was something I could not fathom. It didn't occur to me then. And I wanted to believe that it was her hand-me-down. To this day, I don't know for sure if it was. Either way, Mrs. Collins was very generous.

Running home with this prize, I tried it on. Mother's reaction was very muted. She was not happy for me. This gossamer, cotton candy pink and white dress with a built-in crinoline slip actually fit me perfectly.

Wearing the dress to the party, I discovered what Cinderella felt like at the Prince's Ball. No one's dress rivaled mine at that event. I was royalty. The title of Majestic Belle of the Ball clearly went to me. The night lives on, even now so many decades later.

After tasting heaven's bounty in the night, my mother woke me the next morning, saying that I had to give the dress away. Since I did not have many parties to go to and since I would grow out of the dress, she reasoned that someone should get some use out of it. Before I was out of bed, she told me she was taking it to Cecilia, two streets away. How she ever thought of Cecilia was a mystery since that girl never visited, and Cecilia never liked me.

While I don't know if Cecilia took the dress, or ever wore it, Mother did not come back with it. Cecilia may not have wanted something used.

There certainly was plenty of room in my closet and none of what I had was worth looking at. I was conflicted. Since I preferred seeing that gorgeous dress hanging in my closet for at least a little while, I figured I was selfish to want to keep it longer. Maybe someone else could dress up as royalty. I was glad I got to be princess, if only for one magical evening.

GROWING PAINS:
LESSONS IN THE SCHOOL YARD

While I liked getting away from the classroom for recess, in mid-winter I didn't look forward to freezing outdoors. One particular day in the 6th grade, the bell rang and I grabbed my oversized, beat up, out-of-style coat. It didn't matter that much, since I was not into fashion. But others were, and I didn't like to be the beacon of bad taste. It was not just the kids on the same bus that could see me, but all the students in the rooms facing the parking lot could see me through windows.

As always, some of the girls were talking about boys in our class. Jane said she liked Paul. "Paul" I shrieked incredulously. "How could you like him? You are so much smarter than he is. What would you ever talk about?" "I like the dumb kind," Jane laughed provocatively. For a while, I pondered the personality changes connected to the physical changes in my classmates.

The cold made it tough to breathe. Though feeling like I was suffocating, I still attempted to run with my friends so I wouldn't look weak. I went too far and found myself on the edge of where the 7th grade boys were playing tough games with each other, pushing and shoving. They were in class with my older brother. I recognized one boy as he stopped me, looked in my face and demanded to know if I was Jerry's sister. Not knowing what was the catch, I looked around in a lame attempt to pretend that I thought he was talking to someone else. Another classmate of my brother's confirmed my identity.

When the boy released his grip on me, he said bluntly to the other boys nearby: "Well, she's not all that homely." While having no doubt who started and spread the rumor, I never mentioned it. It was understandable. In that town, a younger sister could be an asset to a brother. She could be a pawn, a trade, or a bargaining chip for a brother to befriend another classmate.

My older brother had to discount me. I was part of the whole home life that had no worthwhile trade. It was a family with no bright future and no bearable present. If no one found me, no one would come to the house. Then no one would discover the awful truth about our darkness.

Free once more from the boy's grip, I saw a friend sitting on the curb. Here was a chance for me to rest and to keep my legs warm with the lower part of my coat. I admired that Amy had the nerve to sit by herself. It made me uncomfortable to see someone disconnected from the group. It reminded me of my real aloneness.

Sitting next to Amy, I inquired what was wrong. What would cause her to be outside the crowd? She told me with pride that she had cramps, already having had her period for a few months. In the sixth grade, I could not imagine how that felt. All I knew was that she was more physically mature than I was. That must make her better, I supposed. Furthermore, while envying the excuse she had for sitting out recess, I worried that I might be stealing her thunder by associating with her badge of female courage. She assured me that my company was welcomed. So we conversed on ordinary things while trying to forget how cold we were.

THE DANCE

At eleven, entering seventh grade, I was old enough to go to the long awaited Friday night school dances held once a month. I had been waiting for that since I entered St. Helena's School in second grade. This was where the BIG kids were. Filled with excitement, I reveled in the knowledge that I had arrived at last.

The first enchanted evening came. As I was getting ready, my mother insisted she was going as well. She invited herself to be a self-declared chaperone. This was not good. While I knew that nobody my age wanted her mother at a dance, mine had a special talent for obnoxious humiliation. All I had to breathe was humiliation. At meals, I drank and ate humiliation. But this was a deeper notch into humiliation hell. I knew that no one at the dance would be safe.

On the ride to the dance , I asserted that there were enough chaperones, so Mother would be wasting her time. After reminding her that she did not like loud music, my undeterred mother was deaf to my meaning. Dad rebuked my lack of appreciation. He spoke abrasively about my attempt at discouraging Mother's admirable intentions.

Unkempt, dressing in mismatched, ill-fitting, out-dated, tattered clothes, Mother in her brash relationship style, asked boys to dance with her. Asked? No, I take that back. She told boys she wanted to dance with them. Overweight and heavy-handed, she afforded the boys no choice. They looked extremely uncomfortable, even pained. I looked away.

Standing and talking with my friends on the other side of the cafeteria/auditorium, I was clear that no one as yet was asking me to dance. Mother appeared to be having a wonderful time dancing like a rainmaker. At times she met someone who didn't know who she was, and she pointed to me. I pretended not to notice, having already gotten as far from her as possible. Thankfully, none in my present circle of friends pointed out the horror that it was **my** mother who was chaperoning and making a fool of herself.

As if things could not implode on me any more, to my shock she brought Teddy to me. She knew his mother. Knowing that he was in my class, she told him to dance with me, emphasizing that I needed a lot of help with boys as she pushed him toward me. Right there in front of me was red-haired, freckled-face Teddy, one of the smartest and nicest boys in my class. Though he was shy, he could get any girl he wanted. Now he looked like a hapless boy with a very twisted arm. Like a puppy dog, Mother was proudly offering me the mouse she just killed. Teddy's spirit was nearly dead from this embarrassment for him. Wincing from the emotional pressure, he tried to smile. What I saw was a boy trying to maintain his best composure.

Any other time I would have loved dancing with him. What an opportunity. What a conflict. I could feel the blood draining out of my face. As best I could, I gently turned down Teddy's forced offer. I gave no explanation, as I tried desperately to disguise my feelings. I quickly disappeared from sight, hiding in a bathroom stall, waiting for the nightmare to end, at least for the dance part of the nightmare to be over.

With no escape, the ride home was worse than the disastrous dance. Mother's story was that she had saved the night by keeping the dance lively. She told Dad that she had more personality than all those young girls did. She was the belle of the ball. What was the matter with everybody else who clearly needed her help? All you had to do was introduce yourself and you would be as popular as she was.

The discussion centered on my ignorance, insolence, stupidity and rudeness for turning down the nice boy. After all, Mother the Martyr was doing me a favor with only my good in mind. Mother had worked very hard to convince Teddy to dance with Mary the Mouse. I had humiliated her with my uppity behavior and lack of gratitude. Teddy was a good boy from a stellar family and I had spurned him. What would his mother think of my mother now, since I had disgraced her? It was no wonder I was a wallflower. The monologue didn't stop. The way I was going I would never find a man.

My father was scornful of my bad behavior and poor decision regarding Mother's help. Both my parents continued to demean me for turning down Teddy's 'invitation.' For years afterward I heard about it.

While I felt that it was true about being mean and ungrateful, my feelings were uncontrollable. Should I say 'yes' when I felt 'no?' Though I had a lot of friends, I talked to no one about the dance, not even Danielle, who loved girl talk.

Going to school the following Monday was one of the hardest things I ever had to do. I could not look Teddy in the eye. Avoiding everyone, I hoped they would all forget somehow what happened on Friday.

Since I loved to dance, I found outlets to satisfy that need. I went to parties that usually included dancing **without** chaperones. Each day after school I danced with the door jam to Bandstand's music on TV. Though it hurt to miss those school dances, I chose to stay away from them all through both 7th and 8th grade.

For many months after the incident, Mother went without me. As Dad left the house to drive Mother to the dance each time, he pointed out that I was "absolutely ridiculous." Only Mother's feelings and viewpoint on anything mattered.

After awhile, Mother stopped going. When that happened, she seemed to resent my stubborn refusal even more. I never asked why she quit the dances. I wondered if someone might have suggested that her aggressive behavior with the boys was inappropriate. Or, maybe some adults thought it weird that I was missing. I doubt it. People were amazingly polite in those days. A more likely reason was that without being able to show me how much better she was than me, Mother eventually lost interest. I preferred not knowing. Whatever stopped her, it had to be something monumental to keep her from doing whatever she wanted.

PART TWO

MOVING INTO TEEN YEARS

ENDINGS AND BEGINNINGS

We three siblings were nearly teens when Dad accumulated enough money to feel that a restaurant dinner a few times a year was not a wasteful use of his resources. On the menu, the restaurant listed chocolate milk as one of the drink options. It did not cost any more. My brothers and I wanted chocolate milk. Mother allowed one chocolate milk and two regular milks with an empty glass.

When it was delivered we were instructed to pour out drink ¼ of the milk in our glass into the empty glass. Then she poured the chocolate milk so that she and we got approximately a fourth of the chocolate milk. A lot was wasted with the chocolate gold flowing down the sides of the glasses. None of us was satisfied with the arrangement of diluted chocolate. Still, we were glad to be eating real food, so no one grumbled in order to avoid being left at home next time.

The summer I graduated from elementary school eighth grade, I was thirteen and looking towards the huge high school in the fall. It was easy to know all fifty of us in our single eighth grade class, since we had been together for many years. I couldn't imagine being in a huge high school.

Every chance I got I borrowed my parents radio so I could listen to the latest top 100 songs. Dad could see that I longed for my own radio and he bought me a gray one for grade school graduation. It was the most prized gift that I had ever received up until then. Not only did it plug in to an electrical outlet, it ran on batteries so I could take it anywhere. Nothing could compare to that gift. I kept it with me and kept the sound low to avoid irritating Mother who hated all "noise," except her own. Guarding it so that Mother did not physically "lose" it, I even took it to bed and kept it under my pillow when I slept. Despite all my precautions, Mother got it and threatened to break it, knowing that it would break my heart. Knowing that nothing was safe no matter what I did, I had to let it go. The first time she took it, I told her that Dad would fix it if she broke it. She said I would never see it again. By the time Dad came home, she returned it as if she had never confiscated it.

Our big vacation that summer was the same as it was for several years. It was one I disliked immensely. How it worked was that for weeks Dad would gather together his list of items for camping. On the big day, we would pile in the car. All of us, except Mother. While we waited, she would make sandwiches to eat on the way, go to the bathroom over and over, and look for some lost item that was not even essential to the trip.

In the car each of us was squeezed in between a hundred items brought to make the 'vacation' civilized. Dad was trying to save money on hotels. Ironically the tent, lantern, cooking utensils, pen knives, outdoor cooking equipment, flashlights and all, cost as much as any motel. Despite the fact that we re-used camping items each year, things got lost or damaged and needed replacing.

At the state park we were assigned a spot with people on either side for a mile each way. It would take hours to set up the tiny tent that held only four people.

Since there were five of us, I'd volunteer to be the one to sleep in the car. The night air was very hard to breathe and after hours of helping with the tent, I was always far overspent. I would sit up on the edge of the back seat and hold on to the front seat for dear life.

While I did enjoy seeing all the trees and walks to the lake, I didn't like the relentless biting flies, varieties of crawly bugs, tree spiders, lack of privacy and lack of friends. After four or five years, it got to be too much trouble even for Dad.

CLOTHES

One piece of clothing that I loved was my shoes. Since we wore uniforms and stockings, the only thing not regulated was the choice of shoes. Having to buy my own, I picked inexpensive ones with the best style for the money. Knowing only terribly uncomfortable ones, I thought discomfort was the nature of all shoes.

Though I always wore flats, for a long time I wore a little black shoe with a narrow heel that flared out at the base. In reality, it was no higher than any other flat shoe, but it felt like it was a tiny bit higher. The other advantage was that it made noise as I walked, especially in the school hallway. Feeling special I walked with a bounce. Walking two and a half miles home from school each day, the heel wore away quickly. So I paid a shoemaker to put rubber at the base. The rest of the shoe began to look shabby after all the walking home and the five flights of steps in school. Lining the shoes with cardboard helped for a while. Not for a moment did I care that the shoes were scuffed and ratty looking.

Lucky for me I had to wear a uniform to school. In high school I had to keep clean my one and only uniform jumper for all four years. Since it had to be dry cleaned, the cost was out of the question. The best I could do was to spot treat the stains. Having only two uniform blouses, I washed them every other day after school.

Mother got ingenious when I hung up my blouses to

dry. She would hide them and then conveniently not remember where. So I had to be extra careful that she did not find my wet blouses after washing them. I usually wrapped them in a towel and hid them under my bed. Since they were long sleeve and 100% cotton, the blouses always showed wrinkles. I was just glad that they were clean when I wore them.

Ironing was a problem since locating the iron was an exercise in futility. Even when found, the iron was problematic with the burnt base, causing rust stains on the clothes.

Underwear, another problem, was something that I learned to handle myself. Since finding things was a perennial game that I resisted playing, I washed, dried and hid underwear, too. The game consisted in who could hide the best and the longest. Of course, I would win some and lose some, but my chances were higher because I would strategize.

My one and only after-school outfit consisted of a sporty red plaid pleated skirt that I matched with a white lace blouse with rips on it. "Well, white goes with anything," I figured. Both items came from the same second-hand store and that was all the two items had in common.

Though I liked the skirt and blouse, my best and longest friend, Barb, said the two styles didn't go together. Really I knew it, but couldn't help it. Saving my babysitting money for bigger thing, like a car, was more important. So I wore my one shabby outfit to football games, school dances, babysitting jobs, forensic club tournaments, and cousins' weddings. It was my after-school uniform.

Barb was seriously impatient and displeased with my lack of fashion sense, and worse, my lack of awareness. Not keeping up with the 'in' look, I felt like I was a bad friend. I did not want to embarrass her as my mother embarrassed me.

To Barb, it likely did not occur to her that my parents would not buy me nice clothes. Seeing me after school without the uniform, Barb would sigh and roll her eyes. We both knew what that meant. She felt I was unmanageable.

Uninterested in hairstyles, clothes or makeup, I was an aberrant teen girl. It was distressing to me that I failed to live up to expectation outside of home, too.

BABYSITTING

Babysitting was my means of cash flow. Well, maybe not *flow* since I saved almost every penny. I had a dream and that was a car in my future, three years before I could take a drivers test.

The babysitting business was good for me. I was good at it. Parents and kids liked me. One parent told another. Soon I had all the business I wanted. In fact, I had more than I could handle. because she was willing, I gave out Colleen's number. Wanting to escape her home life, she wanted the money, though for different reasons. She saw marriage as her escape.

A strange phenomenon started as I began the babysitting career. It was a phenomenon that would continue until I went away to college. Every chance she got, my mother answered the phone before me and told the parents that she would do a better job than I could.

One day my mother told me that at the shopping center she met one of the many parents of children I babysat. She breezily told me that she informed Mrs. Anderson that I stole things on a regular basis.

Horrified, I ask why she lied about me. "Now, I know full well that I have a lot of faults, but that isn't one of them, so why would you say something like that?," I said in a hurt voice, loud enough for my father to hear just outside the room. Mother explained that Mrs. Anderson raved about me. She thought I was such a fine, responsible teen. "I did not want Mrs. Anderson to think I'm prejudiced in your favor." Mother explained. "I don't want you to get a big head."

As my Dad walked past my room, I looked to him for consolation. His demeanor spoke clearly that Mother's conversation was perfectly rational and sensible.

My mother did take some of my babysitting jobs from me. Unperturbed, I figured that I had enough to spare. My only concern was about what other terrible things she was telling people. I could not dwell on it. I had all I could do to get through the day. That was one more thing to stuff down, all the while knowing there would be more to suppress. I was good at that.

Truth was a casualty of our whole family life. The family lived the lie that mother was normal, while dodging the fallout from the lie. Everyday I experienced silent outrage and quiet powerlessness. There was no recourse. Nothing I said or did made any difference. Knowing that I couldn't dwell on all the emotional pain, I put it out of my mind.

SUPPORTIVE FRIENDS

The adjustment to high school with a total student body of 1,250 was enormous. Ninth grade was the transition year for my grade school friends to be thrown in with 400 ninth graders from a wide variety of neighborhood Catholic schools. The sheer numbers were staggeringly hard to grasp. We freshmen went from being in the same classroom all day to being in a multitude of classes all in different rooms on five floors, rushing between bells, carrying   a load of books.

From second grade I had been with mostly the same people in the same school building, only moving once a year to another classroom. Back then, we sometimes had the same teacher each year, but we usually were in a different room for each grade level.

There were no grade school classmates that I disliked. Now that we were scattered into one of eight groups according to test results, only a handful of my friends were with me.

Our Catholic high school was a co-ed experiment. It had opened its doors just a year before I started. Catholic high schools in the Philadelphia area and mostly around the country were all male or all female, not both. I liked co-ed classes since I saw no reason to lose half my friends, the male half.

Everyone felt the pull of the new order with freshmen coming from nine different grade schools all getting completely rearranged. It felt like being a piece of lettuce in a salad spinner.

Naturally nothing was ever the same, but I didn't expect the radical difference that high school would bring. It opened me to the realization that in another setting, people respond differently. Friends who were leaders in the little classrooms of grade school were not so self-expressed anymore.

Once-popular girls looked downright shy and were now hardly noticed in the crowd. Most of the strong personality types never surfaced again in the larger sphere, since there was far more competition.

Having nothing to lose myself, I forged on with my low self-esteem intact, with no major identity change. Though it was an adjustment, I learned that I could swim in a larger pond. The big shift was the loss of so many familiar friends who were with different groups of classes. All of us were navigating new territories. We were discovering new friends who themselves were trying to adjust.

Within a few months I was invited to a party attended by many of the guys and girls who shared the same classes with me. There were far more guys in my class than girls. The imbalance worked fine.

First, being surrounded with the brainiac students was a perk. Surely, a mistake had been made putting me in there. All the time I was hoping not to be discovered and dismissed as less than these smart people, I was grateful I was there.

While there were 54 in each class, there were only twelve of us girls for two of the four years. We became close. Even when the groups were rearranged in junior and senior years and there were only half of the same set of girls, the previous half kept going to parties with us.

Still, I missed Barb, my grade school friend, who was moving with a different group all four years. Not having the same social life with those in her classes, she continued her relationship with me.

To my new group I shared about my vivacious, fun-loving friend Barb and enrolled them in including her. Joining us as the only one outside our classroom circle, Barb was the happy exception made in our tight group. We created sleepovers, dances, and parties as a group. Thankfully, it never had to be at my house.

At the parties, I knew that this was the place to be. Feeling very fortunate, I was not sure why I was accepted, outside of the fact that I was in the same academic group.

When some of the girls held sleepovers, we stayed up all night laughing. Valued and accepted, I was free just to be. At times, I was the cause and center of the entertainment. Imagine that. I could be funny. With them, I was. Who knew? With my friends I emerged stronger. They brought the best out in me, and I appreciated it. Fresh bonds were born. Eventually, the new social group got even more connected, more solid. Emotionally, I was buoyed from that inclusion.

While we had parties and friendships with the guys, the bond was closer with the group of us girls who stayed together socially for all four years. Each friend provided an anchor that held me from drifting on my personal sea of near despair.

As a group, we did not all look the same. Some were tall, some short, some heavy, and some thin. While a few came from money, most of us came from middle to lower class families. None of that was ever a factor. When we were together, we were one. There was no backbiting, no judgments. I experienced only the interchange of friendship.

Like a doorway to a new world, I traveled the high school path with a new set of interesting and engaging people, along with those who became my closest friends. Their approval made me appreciate that there was more to life than my family. These high school friends came from miles around, not knowing my family, or my home life. They were in different parish churches. Best of all they were life nourishing. With these peers, I was liberated, having no thoughts of my family. Inclusive, my classmates discussed interests, and freely shared. While I was with them, Quasimodo did not exist.

Still, did I love myself? Not a chance. Glad that I could get by, I felt lucky. Wondering why others couldn't tell that I was insignificant and worthless, I thought they must be incredibly generous to accept me, or exceptionally blind. Unable to understand it, I just wanted to enjoy every minute that I had before someone found out I didn't deserve them.

After I moved to another state for college, those that stayed locally met occasionally for a little while. Staying near home, Barb continued going to the social gatherings. She was the bridge between my high school friends and me for some months. Meanwhile, I was off making additional friends in college.

Friends meant everything to me. Thoroughly enjoying

people, I took any love I could get anywhere I could get it. I did not know why people loved me. I was just glad they did. Throughout life, caring friends have been there for me. And they have allowed me the privilege of supporting them. Love has healed my wounds.

Relationships continue to be a source of abundance and joy. That has been true throughout my life. Even those I think of as acquaintances have come through in times of need. Love lurks even in unlikely places.

FAITH

There was a lot of talk about faith at church and school. Part of it was incomprehensible to me. Already I had experienced faith in things that did not turn out, like the sister that turned out to be a brother. Every time my mother was hospitalized, I had faith that someday she would get well. So I experienced often a broad gap between faith and the outcome.

When our high school football team played against the other Catholic schools in our division, the school was led in prayer before rallies, imploring God to take our side. God taking sides? Skeptical of why God would care, I wondered what difference would it make to the world. Sure, it made a difference to the players and to school pride, but what about the other school that was petitioning God for them against us?

Because of the boundaries of where they lived, my cousin Pat went to the rival high school. Since there was a football game every autumn weekend somewhere, I knew God had to be hearing pleas all over the country, maybe the world. How would He decide? Did some people pray better, longer or harder than others? Were some people more worthy inherently? If so, why did the same teams both win and lose at different times? How did this favoritism fit with an all-loving God?

Remembering the bible passage about the Israelites being God's chosen people, and thinking that the Catholic Church is the One, True, Holy Church I could see that favoritism was rife in the hearts of people. I doubted God played favorites. If God did take sides, I wouldn't much care for that kind of God.

Still, I felt disappointed in the priests for leading us in the charade, wondering if they had convinced themselves that God could be supplicated for sports. Figuring that the priests were playing a psychological game over us, I did not like being used.

As much as anyone, I wanted our team to win. So I sat in the stands and cheered them on. When our team won, I was ecstatic. When they lost, I was sad. At the same time, I felt the outcome had nothing to do with God. When we lost, I knew there was another team that was celebrating their win over our team. That was life.

MY BEST FRIEND'S MOTHER

Throughout elementary school, my friend, Barb would walk a mile to my home to see me. Honestly, I never knew why she did that, but I was honored and grateful that she chose me to visit. Since it was uphill to get to her home, I almost never walked to her home just to see her, though I did a few times. Uphill walking was especially difficult for breathing.

As soon as high school started, I walked from school five days a week ten months a year for three years in all kinds of weather. It was not my choice to walk two and a half miles carrying many heavy books from school each day. I managed to do it, even when I had great difficulty standing upright, much less walking, often facing wind, rain, sleet and snow.

At times the air was so cold and the snow was so high that I could walk on top of several feet of snow. Always I carried books that weighed almost as much as I did.

Barb's home was the half way mark that I had to pass. Whenever she was walking with me, Barb always invited me to visit her oasis. Feeling unworthy of the invitation, I rarely stopped in, though I did on occasion when it was bitter cold and Barb encouraged me, probably knowing I was in physical distress.

When I did visit, Barb's mother had cocoa and cupcakes ready for her, and cheerily greeted me with the same treats. Mrs. Bowers would tell me to stay as long as I liked. Usually, not wanting to intrude, I would leave quickly, feeling I didn't want to overdo my welcome.

Both her mother and Barb smiled at my delight when I said: "Wow, you have *real* butter." My parents only bought margarine. For my part, I was profoundly impressed with how this mother of four nurtured her family, while keeping an immaculate home.

Mrs. Bowers was too young to be a grandmother like Danielle's caretaker. She did not appear controlling like Judy's mother. For Barb's good fortune, I was happy for her. And I accepted that it wasn't my life. I could not allow myself to desire it to be any other way for me. It took too much energy just to get through the day.

My parents could have sent me to public school where a bus would have left me off in front of school. For them, it was not an option since only a Catholic school would suit their religion.

Later in life my mother told me she felt guilty for having put me through that long walk. Never did I tell my parents how hard it was for me. I told Mother that I knew she did her best.

MORNING

As a freshman I needed to do well in Sr. Anita's class. She thought favorably of me. Not wanting her to know that her class was actually challenging, I was unsure that I could keep up since I could not study at home. Latin was hard to fake.

My bedroom was unfit for studying. No one went into the bedroom area until they had to since the bedrooms were unheated. In the cold weather, that part of the house felt like a walk-in freezer. Dad's reasoned that the cost was too high to heat the three bedrooms. In the rest of the house, Mother's ever-present self was threatening my study time. Whatever I was doing, she had a better idea.

She insisted that I was too interested in reading. Scornful of me for "always having my nose in a book," she knew that reading was my escape. Good grades counted for nothing. Mother was sure I was wasting time. Instead, I could be doing her endless tasks such as scrubbing the floor, cleaning the refrigerator, or any domestic job, none of which she would do.

For example, she waited until it was actually raining before she would order me to get clothes off the line. Those were the same clothes I was ordered to hang on the line. Besides the discomfort of cold rain, Mother knew that it was harder for me to breathe on rainy days.

Though Dad bought a dryer at last, Mother would not use it as long as there were young slaves living in the house. After all, those kids needed to do something to earn their expensive keep.

My brothers were harassed, too. Yet, somehow she was more incensed at my time-wasting endeavor. Mother told me I reminded her of her awful, older sister who did quiet things while long-suffering Mother did all the work. At least that was her Cinderella story. I saw no trace of that left, if hard work was ever in her past.

On a day that I had a big Latin test, in the wee hours of the morning the exam was on my mind. I had more trouble sleeping than usual. Wondering if I'd have enough time to study in homeroom like I usually did, I remembered I had to do algebra homework then. "Well, maybe in History class," I thought.

On this bitter cold night, my only blanket was exasperatingly wrapped around the sheet, preventing anything from covering me adequately. It was my fault that I could not get warm and comfortable since I slept restlessly and I never found time to make the bed. Noticing the dust clinging to the open springs on the bunk above me, I held on to the coils, trying to breathe while feeling like I truly could die.

Struggling every second, it was very painful to both inhale and exhale. Though it felt like no air was moving in me, I couldn't stop breathing no matter how hard it was. Physically and emotionally, I felt there was no exit. While I could not be sure I would get another breath, I noticed that I did not care. This had happened many times before. I survived, simply observing what was happening. I knew I had no control. It would be easier if I did not see morning, but it was just my luck that I would have to press on and keep living. Enduring through the night, it was long and exhausting. I was tired of it all.

Drifting off to sleep, I was in a sitting up position, as usual, since it was too hard to lie down. I dreaded the morning when the loud radio at 6:30 AM would shake me up. It would jolt my senses like an electric fence. In order to turn it off I had to get up out of bed and run to my parents' room, which I could reach quicker than my brothers. My parents always got up first and set the alarm. Getting up meant running through the freezer of a house before I was psychologically ready. It was diabolical.

On this particular morning, my mother woke me up. She came in my room humming at first, then singing when I did not respond. It was dark out. I looked at the clock to see it was 4 AM. Oh, I had slept about 2 hours after another hideous night trying to survive in the Artic. With no energy in my voice, I begged my mother to come back at 6:30 when I had to get up. She pretended not to hear and did a dance for me. Though I heard her moving around, thankfully I could not see it. I clapped weakly. Mother kept talking after I pulled sheets over my head.

FIRST DATE

"A boy is calling you," my 11-year old brother shouted as he handed me the phone. "Hi George," I said in a hush into the phone as my parents paid attention. "Thanks, I'll let you know," was all I could say.

George asked me out for Saturday night. While I was very flattered, I was terrified of the work it would take to get decent clothes, to get the house straightened, and to get my head together. The details were staggering. Unsure that it was worth the effort, I did not know what to do.

My parents overheard my cryptic words and wanted to know. I told them about the offer, hoping they would say that I was not old enough to go out. "Someone asked you out?" they exclaimed in amazement. "Well then, you must go." "But I am only 14," I protested, knowing how my words contradicted my role as an obstinate teen. "In the past, girls got married at 14," my father pointed out sternly. Obviously, I was not living up to the present requirements, much less the past history of womanhood.

My parents let me know there very well might not be another chance for me. Better take it while it's hot, they figured.

Then the real problems started. George wanted to go to a movie on a double date. His older brother, Bob, and Bob's new girlfriend, were going with us. A Saturday night movie was a huge deal, especially a first date. Following the movie, we were going out to have a late snack at the diner.

The first problem was what to wear. Since I did not know his brother's date, I couldn't ask George what the other girl was going to wear. I figured it would be fairly casual.

However, in order for it to be a date, a girl had to be uncomfortable, like wearing high heels. Also, she had to wear a girdle, even if she had an inverted waistline like mine. What did I know of practicalities? I just knew the rules.

While I was babysitting twice each weekend and delivering magazines once a week, I wasn't intending to spend it on nice clothes. In this case, I decided I needed to spend a little money on heels.

Money was not the only challenge. Size was an obstacle. Shoe stores did not sell size 4 ½ heels. When I told enough friends of my dilemma, someone told me that the shoes displayed in the shoe shop windows were smaller than normal.

After searching every day after school, I found a shop with display shoes that the owner was willing to sell. I was elated that something fit reasonably.

The sample pair of heels was size 5. Since even the smallest shoes were too big, I stuffed them the toes with cotton. It was still uncomfortable and tricky to walk.

The shoes were very faded, so I got them half price. The original color had been some kind of indefinable plum. The fading made it look very strange. It was a color that could not match anything in anybody's closet. But they were unmistakably heels!

Well, even I knew that one should not wear heels with my only skirt, that red wool plaid pleated one that was inappropriate to be worn anytime after winter, even though I did on any other occasion.

So I borrowed a straight skirt from a classmate who brought it to school. It was Julie's favorite, a royal blue skirt. She thought it could fit me. While it was supposed to hug the butt, it just hung on me. Knowing that I was entering adulthood, I was thrilled that it was so stylish.

Thinking I needed a blouse, my mother 'found' one for me. Her favorite place to obtain free items explained the stain on the blouse. Even when I got a birthday gift from Mother, it came from her dumpster diving.

The blouse she wanted me to wear was a vivid salmon color, a blend of pink and orange. The collar made it quite sporty as opposed to the dressy skirt. I knew that nothing matched, but my mother would not hear of my rejecting the blouse. Now I hoped that I could just get through this coming awkward evening. Knowing that no one could look as mismatched as I was, I prayed that the other girl in this double date would not be too dressed up or stylish.

Unused to walking hesitantly and cautiously with the limitations of a straight skirt and heels, I wanted to practice walking. There was no time due to the rush to fix up the house. I could not let George see this clutter.

Since Mother would mess up the living area as soon as

I straightened it up, my focus was on cleaning up my own room rather than the rest of the house. It made no rational sense, because I knew that George wouldn't be coming in my room. I just had to do something to make one thing nice.

If she suspected what I wanted, Mother would mess things up even more. So I waited until just before my date to clean up the living room as best I could before Mother noticed the improvement. Though exhausted from all the cleaning, I shoved all the items out of the tub in order to shower. Spending all day moving mountains of debris, somehow I made it on time.

George didn't act like he noticed the surroundings. He shook hands with my parents and just beamed at me. It was probably his first date, too. Walking uneasily toward the door in my heels, I was already feeling the pain. Why did I have to be such a shrimp, I chided myself, as if I had any control over size.

Just then, my younger brother made a surprise appearance. "So, you're going out in THAT?" His attempt to be amusing only reinforced the sick feeling I had about the clothes.

Getting to the car, George opened the back door and scooted inside after me. A beautiful girl sat in the front next to his brother. Aghast, I had the words: "Oh no" ringing in my ears over and over. She was wearing a black crepe evening dress. Told that we were going to an ordinary movie theatre, I was shocked to learn that George had wanted to surprise me. We were going across town to a giant fashionable theatre. From friends I had heard about the chandeliers, the huge foyer, the formal doormen, and the elegant stairway. I wanted to run back inside and hide. I wanted to at least change clothes. Then I remembered I didn't have any better clothes.

Before the date, I had terrible nightmares of me walking outside in my pajamas. In some dreams, I was walking naked in public. On this date, I realized that I was living that nightmare. Throughout the night I was in emotional anguish. When we went to the diner, I couldn't eat. I felt that I was a party pooper.

Amazingly, George asked me out again despite how uncomfortable and uptight I was. He pursued me all through high school, even though I swore off that kind of proper dating. It was way too much trouble getting ready and I was way too confronted on a date.

After that, George and I had a running dialogue. He would ask me out for a Friday or Saturday night and I'd say: "No. I am too busy." He would say: "How's 8 PM on Friday?" I'd insist that it was unworkable. He'd say: "I'll see you at 8 on Saturday" and walk away fast. I'd yell after him: "I won't be home."

On most Friday and Saturday nights I was occupied with babysitting at some other family home. Yet, on the few nights that I wasn't babysitting, George was there at my house. In the warm weather nights, he would bring vegetables that he grew. That pleased my father. Not wanting to be rude or rejecting, I'd sit and watch TV with George in our living room, feeling uncomfortable.

My brothers assured me that George never came over when I was out. So I am positive that George checked my schedule with my mother and father who were both planning my wedding with him from the moment those three met.

VISITING THE HOSPITAL

Mother was in a mental hospital soon after I had finished freshman year in high school. Neighbors called the police and complained that Mother was again doing strange things. It could have been the dumpster diving, it could have been the sleeping outdoors, it might have been something I was not told, or it could have been a mix of things.

Men in white coats arrived. Dad insisted that she be taken to a private hospital, not the state hospital that Mother, on previous stays, had objected to.

There was a high out-of-pocket cost for the private place. Dad never paid a high price for anything before, and he must have thought it was necessary. He considered it a family disgrace for her to go to the state hospital, as if paying high prices could possibly dispel the stigma of mental illness, even a little. Evidently, Dad didn't seem to think Mother's actions were a disgrace. It was just that being at that hospital was shameful.

It seemed like a long time before Mother was allowed to have visitors. When the first day arrived, my brothers and I dressed up in our Sunday best. Admittedly, that wasn't much.

Once inside the gates, Dad drove up the long driveway. It was a sunny June afternoon full of promise. We were very impressed with the sheer size of the building. It had interesting turrets; immense towers, massive doors, and fascinating trim, making it look like an aged fortress.

What I liked was the pretty grounds with abundant flowers and well-trimmed bushes. They were unlike the bushes outside our house that grew out of control, just like everything else at our place.

While there was a lot of space on the hospital grounds, not one person was outside. No one was enjoying it.

Walking inside, the very thick, cold, stone walls made the place feel acutely dark and cheerless. Directed to the top floor, we were climbing the steps hearing the sounds of screaming all around us. They were especially loud on the top floor when we got there. The high and low pitched sounds of moaning signaled real pain and anguish. My skin was covered with goose bumps.

Urgently, I wanted to tell the unseen screamers and moaners that I would buy them something with my allowance if they would quiet down. "Why didn't the staff help the patients?" I questioned my silent father. Evidently they could not. The sounds were so very disturbing that I wanted to run. This was my new definition of hell. "Oh my God, I have to stay and listen to this? This may be worse than Mother's usual uncontrollable screaming because this so pulls at my heartstrings."

For a while we waited on a stark, long, hardwood chair that seated all of us. In this big room, the uncomfortable seats like ours were lined up against the walls. The center of the room was empty, giving it a lonely, eerie feel.

Dad spoke with a nurse and then disappeared through a door. Noting the people sitting around, I observed that most seemed depressed, or bored. "They must be sad that the relative for whom they are waiting is locked up in this medieval building," I surmised.

Uneasy with the whole situation, my attempt to soothe myself was to discuss, in an effort to figure out the unfathomable. Engaging my brothers, I speculated on whether Mother's behavior was deliberate, or whether she was helpless in the face of it. My view was that if she could have stopped it, she would have been smart enough to clean up her act before this incarceration befell her.

My 11-year old brother was having none of it. "It is deliberate, I am sure," he asserted. "She knows what she is doing and does it for the attention. She just got caught this time," he continued.

Not so sure myself, I looked to my 16-year old brother. He showed no partiality to either view. He may not have cared what was the cause. Just the reality was enough to grasp.

A vibrant and stunning woman talked to the nurse behind the desk, and to everyone in general. She announced this was her 21st birthday.

In awe of her energy and beauty, I wondered who she might be visiting. Was it a mother, a sister, a father or a brother that she came to see? Instantly, I liked her and envied her. "Even when I am 21, I'll never be that accomplished and that attractive," I realized. Her makeup was flawless. In her tall, perfectly developed frame, her dress was exceptionally elegant. "She must be rich since she has it all," I murmured to myself.

How generous of her to visit someone else when it is such an extraordinary day for her. Now she was an official adult, she could be out drinking. Yet, here she was bringing joy to a loved one.

Strangely, no one responded to her announcement or seemed to care that it was her special birthday. It was the Big Day of Liberation that every young person longs for. Still, others appeared indifferent to her speech.

Wanting to approach her, I was held back by shyness. This was a confident, charismatic, extraverted, intelligent young lady. Why would she want to talk with somebody like me? I was grateful that she continually talked about many intellectual subjects. No one else had anything to contribute, so she was the main event. Her talk kept my restlessness at bay.

Just then, a nurse came out escorting Mother. Walking slowly, she was not her belligerent self, nor was she a new model mother, the one I dreamed of, the fantasy one that was kind and caring. It was sad seeing her zombie demeanor. She was looking very defeated, as if she met her match and had been beaten at her game. It was like seeing a puppy that had been whipped into submission and nothing was left. Suddenly, I thought of Gertrude Stein's quote: "There is no there, there."

Mother had nothing to say outside of vaguely answering dull questions. "How's the food?" I inquired. This was usually of utmost importance to Mother. She seemed apathetic. "Have you made any friends?" She scoffed at the absurdity of the question.

I was the only one asking. Mother didn't want to talk

and no one in our family did either. The constant pitiful screaming outside the room unnerved us all. I felt sorry for Mother. "No one would want this," I thought, vowing to never allow this disease to get hold of me. I could tolerate anything, but this.

While Mother was uncharacteristically quiet, the wild voices kept echoing behind the walls. "How does Mother stand the sounds of pain from so many others?" Then I wondered how often Mother was one of those voices before being drugged up like she was now. It was not like her to submit easily. Visions of forced restraints made me shudder.

The sensational young lady's voice was still a powerful force in the room as she spoke of literature, history and philosophy. She knew everything, it seemed. I admired her knowledge, talent, and self-assurance.

Turning back to Mother, I asked if she knew who could be the patient for whom this sweet young lady was waiting. Immediately Mother stated that she knew 'Susie.' Mother's distain for her was palpable. "Susie is no visitor and she's not sweet. She is a patient who many times has gone through shock treatments." In fact, Susie **never** has visitors.

Now I was the one stunned, shocked beyond belief. "Maybe this is how shock treatment feels," I thought. My world was rocked. My senses were reeling. "No, it can't be. How can this be possible? No. This cannot be true. It was natural for Mother to be very mean, but why would she say that of this beautiful woman?"

Though Mother was very certain of her statement, I did not want to accept it. I could not assimilate the thought of this lovely lady with my experience of how

Mother expressed mental illness, nor how the unseen screamers and moaners expressed it behind the walls.

Looking at the possibility Mother was right, I noticed that while Susie behaved appropriately, there were two similarities with Mother. They both talked incessantly and neither wanted meaningful interaction.

Yet, Susie's talk was delightful. "Could people with different personalities suffer the same illness? How does that illness reveal itself in different people? Is it possible that not all the mentally ill are like my mother?" I contemplated this with no resolution.

No patient came out to see Susie that day and no visitor came in to see her. The staff paid no attention to her exciting monologues. I was baffled. She was still there when all visitors had to leave. Logic forced me to question my reality. Susie's lack of visitors made me wonder what could have happened in her life. Maybe mental illness doesn't require something happening to cause it. Marveling at the sheer perseverance and determination it took to primp and perform for such a poor audience, I thought she would make a splendid actress if ever she got well. No longer did I trust assuming anything. No matter what her story, I felt very confused and conflicted about Susie.

Hugging Mother good-bye, I hoped she would become normal, knowing that it would take a miracle. Leaving the hospital behind, we walked back to the car in warmth and sunshine under a cloudless sky. Continuing to feel profoundly sad for Susie, and cautiously hopeful for Mother, I felt absolutely grateful for my freedom.

Outside, I lingered a moment in the direct sunlight

156

that was lost to the inmates. Before sliding into the backseat with my brothers, I waved to the blank windows of the hospital in case someone could see. Possibly they could have a moment of virtual relief from their limited existence. No one looked out.

Mother was released soon after our visit. We visited late in her stay since she was not well enough to see us any earlier. Three weeks was all the insurance would pay for any mental hospital. It was only a partial payment since she was in a fancy place, not fully covered.

When she came home, as always there was an angry backlash. Mother claimed she was put away against her will. It was everyone else's fault. Insisting that there never was anything wrong with her, Mother was enraged about the bad treatment at the hospital. Evidently, the higher cost did not guarantee Mother a better experience.

Since Dad was gone all day at work, Mother took out her fury on her children. School was out and provided no refuge. We three again found our separate ways to hide out for the better part of every day. We were experienced at disappearing. Whenever we were under the same roof, Mother wanted us to be as miserable as she was.

While she was away, I had straightened up, cleaned house, and cooked meals as best I could. Mother cluttered it down to her level of comfort within the hour. The house was a mess again as she 'reorganized' my attempt at de-cluttering to a jumble of rubble. Soon we were back to moldy food in the fridge and grass soup for dinner.

I was right to be cautiously hopeful. Her return proved clearly that there was no hope.

THE TREASURED STATUE

For observation and tests on severe and unsightly eczema on my neck, arms, hands, and legs, I was reluctantly incarcerated in the hospital at age 15, a sophomore in high school. It was obvious all my life that something needed to be done and it was getting worse. My hands broke out and oozed when I turned a knob. Doing dishes exacerbated the problem, though it never got me out of doing them. The required school stockings irritated the creases in the back of my knees that were already sore and itchy. Getting stocking off my legs ripped them even after carefully peeling stockings off the sores that seeped through the mesh and congealed. Every school day made the sores worse.

Skin and Cancer Hospital was, at the time, in a seedy side of downtown Philadelphia, not an easy commute for my stay-at-home mother. It required taking a bus and a train, so I would see her only on occasional Saturdays when my father could bring her.

Hating any hospital, I especially despised one I couldn't leave. Prison could not have been worse for me, I thought. Fighting boredom, I sought some fun. Quickly getting to know everyone on the floor, I was tempted to go to other floors. The problem was that I had no access to the clothes and shoes I wore there. For the convenience of doctors, I had only a hospital gown and my underwear.

The turnover was rapid and I prided myself on

keeping up with the comings and goings of everybody on the floor. I knew the nursing staff schedule, each of their children's names and their marital situations. It wasn't hard since there were a limited number of staff. Daily, I visited the 80 patients in all the rooms on that floor. Practiced at listening to my mother constantly, I listened to the patients and was privy to their heartbreaks and their triumphs.

Pat, a lady down the hall received a basket of goodies that included a stuffed pink cat. Unable to leave her room, Pat immediately sent word through the nurses that she wanted me to visit right away. When I arrived, she insisted that I take the fluffy cat toy that she said she didn't want. Gratefully, I cherished the cat until it fell apart many years later. It accompanied me through college and into my first apartment as a reminder that I was loved.

One way I survived was having my prized radio with me. Since I was the youngest one in that hospital, I got away with a lot. With the permission of my three roommates, I would play music and dance around the room.

There was too much food and milk at mealtimes, so I kept extras on the outside ledge of the window nearest to my assigned bed. Being winter, the milk froze. There were also many stored snacks. The other three in my room saw what I was doing and gave me their extras. Soon it became impossible to eat or drink all the spares, but it was comforting to have them. There was always something to share when friends came to visit.

Only one person in my room, Eileen, had company and her family brought her éclairs. I had never heard of éclairs. Soon Eileen's father brought one for me. It was a piece of heaven.

Since I was on the top floor, I discovered that pouring water down to the pavement below made me laugh hysterically. Looking north and south to make sure no one was coming, I poured the water. Hearing the splashing sound below was a victory for me. The fear that dropping it might be dangerous or illegal made it even funnier. Then I'd go about my mischief with the glee of a hungry dog finding a bone. I wondered if I was going crazy and I didn't even care. Any excuse to laugh was addictive and nothing could stop me.

Besides Eileen, among the others occupying the same hospital room was Sara, an 80-year-old Jewish woman. Though she intrigued me with her blue hair elegance, it was painful to watch her misery. Sara had a death wish and that repelled me. That was one more reason to spend much of my time meeting others out of the room.

In an effort to comfort Sara, I asked about her background. Surprisingly, she was the youngest of her family members. Not only her parents, but also her husband and siblings preceded her in death. Even her son had died in the Korean War. Though it had happened many years earlier, Sara choked up in sharing the loss of her son.

When my parents visited there were no gifts for me and none expected. There was no gift for two of my roommates.

However, my mother gave Sara something that was wrapped in a brown institutional paper towel. Obviously, she had just wrapped it from the paper towel dispenser in the public restroom. Due to my mother's strong urging, Sara took the awful looking object and opened it. To my amazement it was my statue of the Blessed Mother. It was the one I received when I made my First Communion. The statue had been one of my treasures since I was six years old and I prized it, even at 15.

Inside the statue was my only rosary with beautiful blue beads that sparkled. I was crushed, saddened and dismayed. Intensely frustrated, I was struck by how ingenious my mother was. Who could fault her for giving a gift to a lonely old lady? How could I ruin it by telling Sara that this was not my mother's to give? I felt I had no right.

Looking at it, Sara gave no clue that she was offended by this Christian symbol. She put it aside and said nothing.

Earlier she had told me that the name Sara meant 'regal.' Certainly she conducted herself with dignity. I was embarrassed that my mother was so insensitive to Sara. Too mortified to say anything, I prayed that Sara would tell me that she couldn't use the statue and give it to me. Everyday, I checked her trashcan to see if she had thrown it away. Sara never mentioned the 'gift' and neither did I. Soon to her disgust, she was dismissed from the hospital while still protesting that she had no family and no place to go. Feeling profoundly sad about her situation, I prayed for her... without my rosary that was inside the statue.

After two weeks, the doctor ordered a routine x-ray for me. My insurance must have allowed for it. The doctor suddenly discovered that I had serious lung problems all along. I was transferred to Temple

University Hospital. There the label 'emphysema' was added to my growing medical file.

For 10 days the huge busy staff at Temple University Hospital ignored me, except for delivering daily pills. The first day I was presented with a recognizable pill for breathing, along with another strange brown pill. Quickly I asked why the brown pill. The nurse said it was for constipation. When I told her I never had constipation, she insisted that I would likely get it there. As soon as the nurse disappeared, I stashed the pill in the trashcan.

That incident reinforced my belief that I had to be responsible for my body. Relying blindly on doctors, or nurses would be dangerous. That insight supported me the rest of my life. Nonetheless, I made errors in judgment, like spending decades denying how serious my lung condition was.

Nothing happened at the hospital to improve my lungs and no information came forth for how to deal with them. I was transferred back to Skin and Cancer Hospital.

Not knowing why I was back there, I was miserable. The patients I knew were already gone. Alarmed that I was missing so much school, life was at a standstill in the hospital. The same skin creams that made no noticeable difference became a travesty to me.

Later, I left the hospital with skin and lungs no better off than before. The hospital released me on exactly the 30th day, matching my father's insurance of 30-day coverage for physical issues. Thank heavens for insurance limits. Too bad the hospital didn't have to show results for a patient's time.

SCHOOL RETURN

When I returned to school after being gone for that month of missing out on my normal routines, I was glad to rejoin my friends and my studies.

Both hospital and school were restricting and constricting in different ways. Both were a world unto themselves with little concern for the ways of the outside world. Each was its own institution, its own closed society. While inside the hospital small world, I had time to look out windows, fascinated with the sidewalk people and the cars going by, pondering where they were going and what they were up to.

School, by contrast, was intense and insular, keeping my attention inside. It felt like I had expanded by experiencing life outside of school. While away, it intrigued me to wonder what other simultaneous realities were going on.

Back in school I thought about the hospital people I met. For a while, I wrote to Pat, the generous pink cat lady, until she stopped responding.

Also, when I returned to catch up with eight different classes of month-long homework, I was expected to complete it all in two days. Though I had been doing all the long-term assignments I had known about, more catch-up assignments were given to me on my first day back. It would take at least two weeks to finish all homework assigned in these various classes.

Anyone absent one day would get two days to

complete one's homework. In my case, no adjustment to the rule was made for an absence of a month. Since I was unable to complete it in two days, I was sent to detention. Rules, I realized did not always make sense.

At the end of that second day back, my name was called for having detention. The boys who often got detention, shouted in disbelief. The buzz went through all the sophomore classes. Detention was filled each day with the same people, mostly the same boys, give or take a few. Those who had detention often were proud of it. They were not the boys in my classes. Now they were suddenly thrilled that someone new to detention would be in their midst.

Some boys who knew me from homeroom, went out of their way earlier to say they'd meet me there. On arriving in after school detention, I was greeted with instant acceptance as they smiled at me. They did not seem insincere or mocking. It did not appear that they wanted revenge on someone who never went to detention. It simply was a novelty for them that I could be punished. Maybe for them it wasn't so bad that they were punished, at least that day.

Happy to get their admiration for a day, I went to detention as one of the guys. Looking around the room, I noticed it was just a classroom like any other. For about twenty of us, it was like study hall, except school was out for everyone else. *Not so bad*, I thought. Though, I never liked losing freedom, I figured that detention wasn't as awful as I feared. Still, I never had occasion to be there again.

The boys never knew why I was there, and I stayed mum. Though I don't know how long that detention experience bought me favor with those guys, it made an impact on all of us. Instead of being upset that I was punished unjustly, I was pleased that my conventional good-girl reputation had changed.

As for the boys who felt that the dullness of detention was only for them, they didn't care why I was there. They were ecstatic that they weren't the only ones that could get disciplined. They wanted to believe that I was like them. So did I. We were each locked in our patterns. While wanting to be someone else, I still didn't have any more real choice in how I behaved than they did.

COLLEGE PLAN

My high school junior year was easier than sophomore year. The dreadful biology class with the forced memorization of every genus of every living thing was OVER. Despite disliking chemistry class, it was a breeze by comparison. French seemed easier than either one of the two previous years of Latin. Of course, I had all the other requirements that every junior has. It was still a full plate.

My father had gone through college and expected that his sons would, too. For Jerry, school held little interest, so he enlisted in the Army as soon as graduation came. Eddie later would choose college, though at the time I was planning my future, he was too young to consider his path.

As a daughter, I was expected to marry, the younger the better, and to have children "the more the merrier." By junior year in high school, the popular thing was to be sporting an engagement ring. Besides wanting to see the world, I had revulsion for marriage and motherhood. Sure that I would turn into my mother as soon as the wedding bells rang, I couldn't let that happen.

Everyday coming home from school, there were college catalogs waiting for me. Side by side, they could have covered the floor of a football field, and I was not even a senior yet. Seriously I examined each possibility: the location, the courses, and the prices.

Ever since starting high school, I had been talking about college.

Three colleges appealed to me. One was Chestnut Hill, the local Catholic Women's College, where my cousin Joan was currently in her junior year. Some of my friends hoped to go there. Surely, I figured that my younger cousin, Judy, would attend that local Catholic college. Upon visiting the college, I was very impressed with the atmosphere. The nuns seemed extremely friendly, much more pleasant than the nuns we had in high school.

Knowing that I had through high school been unable to study at home in a safe atmosphere, I realized I needed a college away from my house so I could focus. If I stayed in the area and came home to the emotional drama, the non-stop noise with the mold and cold, I wouldn't get through the academic rigors.

The second consideration was St. Mary's in New Mexico. While I liked the course offerings, the best part of it was the weather. How wonderful it would be to float free from the freezing cold all winter. Yet, it would take me a long time to get back and forth to Philadelphia. I was still attached to friends and believed I should be loyal to family and relatives, most of whom lived nearby.

The last consideration was the College of Mt. St. Joseph. It was in a neighboring state. That meant that I could make it home for Christmas. It wouldn't be terribly far to go for summer break. "What if I miss my friends, especially Barb?" I panicked. "What if I can't take the loneliness?" I needed to be close enough to come home in a reasonable amount of time. St. Mary's was too far. Chestnut Hill was too close.

After narrowing the choices, the next step was to see whether I could get any earnest funding, since I never heard about scholarships. So I planned to approach Dad knowing that he believed college was wasted on females. Neither his wife, nor his three sisters, nor his six sister-in-laws ever went to college.

What I could exploit was his doubts that his daughter had what it took to get a husband. "College could buy me time to find someone" was my premise. "Take her, she's mine" really was Dad's attitude. His lack of confidence in me could turn to my advantage.

Still, this would not be an easy sell. He was tightfisted with money. Besides, for him my only purpose was to have lots of Catholic babies. And who was I to be asking for such huge funding? Why would I need to go to college?

So I took his mind off the 'should she' or 'shouldn't she' conundrum. Instead, I pointed out the total costs of College Hill verses the total costs of Mount St. Joseph. College Hill, the local college, would cost just as much for tuition as Mt. St. Joseph would cost for the tuition with room and board. It would be cheaper than local college, keeping me home and feeding me.

Dad agreed with my math. Reluctantly, but generously, he agreed to pay my tuition. I still do not know why he agreed. I have always been grateful. It changed my life.

TELEPHONE

Though I was wearing the same uniform to high school every day, I did have a few clothes that found their way to my closet by my junior year. One dress I actually bought myself. If my classmate Priscilla's mother had not been the saleslady, I would not have bought it. I felt obligated. When I got home with it, my parents made me feel it was a mistake for me to spend my own money. OK, the dress was ugly, even by my low standards. I had been taken in my Mrs. Moore gushing over how great I looked in it. Though I did not believe it, I still bought it.

Also, when I was 16, I actually sewed a whole dress myself from a pattern. That time, my friend Sarah went with me when I was buying the fabric.

Disapproving of the bright colors I liked, Sarah encouraged me to buy a dark blue gingham type material that was definitely not my taste. While I didn't know my taste, I knew enough that this did not reflect me. Thinking I was wrong to have my taste, I listened to my friend. After all the work on that dress, I wore it only once.

Except for the dress I made, and the sporty plaid skirt with the frilly white blouse, what hung in my closet Wherever Mother had found clothes, it was not in a clothing store. To my parents, buying clothes was an unnecessary expense and they knew how to avoid it.

Mother put clothes in my closet that were even more

uncomfortable and unflattering than the one outfit I wore everywhere after school in all seasons.

In my closet, what was not a trash find, or a hand-me-down, came from a really seedy second-hand shop. My clothes were poorly fitted and poorly styled. They hung there, taking up space. That is why I stuck with my one outfit. Even if it was a design disaster, it was familiar.

When one of my girlfriends called, she had serious news. Since Mother was raging at me, I could barely hear Sandy. It was nothing new that Mother was screaming at me. She hated it when I was on the phone. This time I knew I needed to pay attention to the call. Sandy was serious about something and I could not quite get what. I said "uh-huh" to soothe Sandy as Mother turned up the volume, blaring her message, demanding that I clean out my closet now.

Mother was more than serious. She was furious. Why did she choose a time when I was on the phone? I knew the answer. There was nothing wrong with my closet because there was next to nothing in it. "What about her own closet, so stuffed that the extras were littered on her floor? What about the rest of the house? It was so unfair," I was thinking as I was trying to gauge how soon I might have to run and listen to my friend at the same time.

As usual, I was embarrassed about being the object of the shouting, but Sandy never seemed to be bothered by the background hyena noises that my mother made. Sandy just urgently wanted me to listen to a story about some classmate's parent. At the same time my own parent desperately wanted me to obey. I teetered on a seesaw between two intensely competing influences.

Mother's demand required an immediate response. Nothing ever changed. She wanted me to clean the oven, do the dishes, get laundry done, etc. It didn't matter the task. It was just intolerable to her that I not be following orders. Anything else was unacceptable. My life had to revolve around her.

Mother came over and yanked me toward my bedroom. I pulled away, all the while holding on to the phone for dear life. She screeched. Constantly, I attempted to keep in the conversation with Sandy, but Mother was like a bull that I had to dodge. I did not want to ask Sandy for clarity since I was sure she had told me already. The cost of inattention was severe.

Still, I had more pressing concerns at the moment. Suddenly Mother charged toward my bedroom. Aware the war was not over, I knew there would be hell to pay. Fortunately, Sandy was ready to get off the phone. I could not remember a thing she said. My hope was that my distracted listening provided some solace for whatever she had on her mind.

When I went to my bedroom, both windows were wide open. Looking outside, I saw my whole miserable wardrobe lying all over the grass. Luckily, I was still wearing my uniform. Since I washed my uniform blouse everyday anyway, I had no worry. Internally, I vowed to wear my uniform even on weekends. Unperturbed, I left the clothes on the lawn. I wouldn't talk about the fact that Mother cleared out my closet in an angry outburst of revenge. Both my parents repeatedly instructed me to pick up my clothes on the lawn. I simply asserted that I didn't put them there. When it was suggested that someone would steal my clothes, I laughed. Life went on as usual.

Two days later, Sandy told me about the funeral of our friend Jean's father. Surprised and hurt, I asked why she didn't tell me about this funeral. Sandy informed me that she did tell me two days ago when she called. It was her assessment that I didn't care about Jean's loss. As I watched her walk away, I marveled that she was so used to my mother screaming that it did not occur to her as a possible distraction to me. There was no allowance for such an attention handicap. Even more, I wondered why it didn't count that on every other occasion I showed that I did care about people. The others in school that went to Jean's father's funeral probably thought the same thing. What was important was I needed to apologize to Jean without revealing why I wasn't there.

Too hurt, I said nothing to Sandy. It was humiliating to try communicating the whole mess. No one appeared to see what was obvious, even visible, right out in the open. People seemed to not see what was going on in my family. Not my friends, not neighbors, not relatives ever seemed to put any clues together. So I pushed on silently thinking it must be my fault somehow. Was it possible I was not a good daughter to my mother? Maybe that's why we did not get along. It felt hopeless to find the key to peace with Mother. What was I missing?

Since I figured that Sandy still loved me, I overlooked this blip on the Friendship Road. Surely, she saw faults she had to overlook in me, too.

Weeks later, someone put my clothes back in my closet without saying a word. It had to have been my father, tired of seeing the clothes sprawled out like so many lifeless bodies. He was the one who was embarrassed by what the neighbors might think. Since I had lost any sense of dignity much earlier, I wasn't as bothered. There were no clothes that I liked. There were none that I really needed, other than what I had to wear to school. It would not bother me to wear my uniform to church since it was better than anything else I had.

DRIVING

The spring after my 16th birthday when the roads were ice free, I turned my attention to learning to drive. Mother did not drive, so I harassed my father until it was easier to teach me than to listen to me.

The day came for the first lesson. Not very confident in this, I made a lot of mistakes. My father was extremely nervous, yet patient, a trait for which I was enormously thankful.

Since his was the only car, he taught me on it. All the while, he worried about keeping the car in one piece. Since I was such a novice, I went through stop signs and red lights. Forgetting to watch speed limits, I drove too quickly, turned too abruptly, and tailgated too closely. While Dad restrained any natural, human impulse to yell, his disapproval was palpable. Teaching my older brother must not have been as hard on him, I supposed.

Miracle of miracles, I passed both the driving road test and the written test the first time out. Dad was surprised and amazed, mixed with relief.

Not long after my driver's license became my most prized possession, I was ready to purchase a car. Dad came with me to share his expertise. We went to one used car lot. For a while we were ignored until one salesman came out. He wanted to know what kind of car I was looking for. Not having studied car types, my only standard was one that worked.

With great authority, Dad led with his idea of negotiating. He stated the amount I had saved in my three and a half years of sacrificing most Friday and Saturday nights to babysitting jobs. He gave the total amount with nothing left over.

"Ah," the salesman said: "I have something right over here." It was a car hidden away. There was no price on it, but the salesman said it was the one for my price. "Take it or leave it" he smiled and stood there, so I did not think I could not speak with Dad alone.

Not having bought a car before, I did not know that I had a right to drive it first. It seemed to be the only car. It was the only lot Dad recommended. Dad thought I should buy this seven-year-old green Chevy clunker. Not seeing any options, I agreed to the price. That left me no money.

After signing the papers, I drove it off the lot. It was not an automatic like Dad's, the one I learned on. This stick shift was one where I was gripped with fear as I drove down the street. I say 'down' the street, which happened to be an extremely lucky direction, rather than up. The car had barely enough gas to start it, so I slid down the street to a gas station. Fortunately, Dad followed in his car. Since I had spent every cent I owned on the car, I had to borrow money from Dad for gas.

Then, I begged him to switch cars for the ride home, so I could safely learn to drive a stick shift on my street rather than on the main highway. When we met back home Dad showed me once the basic shifts while the car was parked in the driveway. Then he told me I was on my own to learn shifting in motion. It took me more tries than I'd like to admit.

176

For weeks I was starting and stalling all the way down the street. I did not feel I could go far without stalling out. Eventually, I got smoother in making the transition between the gears. Going from an automatic to a shift car felt like a steep learning curve. Dad's car had only one petal to worry about. Mine had two. My jerky, fast motions between the petals and the gears did not help. "Did anyone else ever make so many mistakes?" "Did the neighbors ever see anyone else look like such a fool?" Sometimes I had to start up my car three times before I got off the driveway. When I asked Dad for help, he told me that he had had enough of teaching. I could not entirely fault him for that.

No one in my home was happy for my car or my freedom, but having a car at school brought privilege. Senior year at school, there were only ten parking spots reserved for students in the staff lot next to the school building. The teachers chose me to have one of the parking spots. Since it was difficult enough to breathe going up and down five flights of steps, I was deeply grateful that I didn't have to walk several blocks as other car owning seniors did.

From turning corners with that Chevy, in senior year in high school I developed muscles that I didn't know I had. I loved that green vehicle that drove like a truck. Having wheels saved me from hunger because in that last year in high school, I ate every night at Louie's Burger Place before I went home. Fast food was a new thing and it did not come along a minute too soon for me.

Over my one year with the car, I gained about 15 pounds, moving from 75 to 90 pounds. I remained thin, but satiated. Of course, part of the reason I added the pounds is because I was no longer walking two and a half miles home from high school.

Business opportunities came with my car. Designing a way to pay for the gas, I figured out how many students I could fit in my car. Reserving free spaces for best friend, Barb, and for my kid brother, that left three more spaces for paying customers. Charging a flat fee of a dollar a week, the three dollars paid in abundance for my gasoline costs. And that car took me to splendid places.

ENCOURAGEMENT... IN A NUN'S GARB

English class was always my favorite, especially when we studied literature. Sr. Augustine was my favorite English Teacher and she taught me in both junior and senior years. She noticed something good about me. It's likely she did that with others, too. Moreover, she told me what she thought.

As the head of the school newspaper, Sr. Augustine requested that some of us in her class write articles to submit for publishing. As a result, she named me Creative Writer, a job that didn't exist before.

Never would I have considered myself worthy of such a post. How perfect. I didn't have to write boring news, I could write **anything.** For two years that is exactly what I did, loving every moment.

Also, I developed a book of quotes for future creative writers to use with possible articles, or to prompt articles. Loving the freedom, I felt an expansion of my interests and strengths. While I took no particular pride in my position as Creative Writer, I took pride in doing my best. Happy that the job would continue, it was bittersweet turning it over to an underclassman, shortly before I graduated.

Besides approving of me through her actions, Sr. Augustine actually told me that I was thoughtful. That description remains with me. Never having heard that before, I didn't want to disappoint. It was a stunning piece of news. I loved Sr. Augustine from that day.

Frequently, I wrote to her through college and visited her years after that. One day, she was no longer at my high school. Sadly, I could get no information on her whereabouts.

PART THREE

MOVING INTO ADULTHOOD

BREAK IN; BREAKTHROUGH

Mother had terrifying physical strength. Up until this day, I have yet to meet anyone who could match her.

On one of the days when she was on the warpath, I went into the semi-protection of my room. Without a lock on my door, Mother banged and pushed against the door until my body barricade was not enough. For such attacks, I would put my back against to door and my feet against the foot of my bed. It always seemed strange to me that doctors referred to sudden breathing problems as 'attacks.' Those were inner attacks. Little did the doctors know about the outer attacks that I had to deal with daily. I would never tell anyone, since it might be my fault that it was happening to me.

Around the time I was getting ready to go away to college, that same thing happened. On one particular day, I couldn't hold Mother out of the bedroom and couldn't get out my open window before she grabbed me, and squeezed my throat. Seeing her ferocious intensity, I could feel the life going out of me. This incident was more violent than usual and the usual was scary enough. Feeling that she could and would kill me, I dug my nails into her arms that were suffocating the life out of me. It wasn't much of a defense, but it was all I could do.

All of a sudden Mother stopped choking me and became very childlike. She could have kept going which would have strangled me. Yet she acted deeply offended that I would do such a horrible thing, as if I had no reason to protect myself at all. It was as if she had awakened from a dream, seen only a part and interpreted it as an attack on her. Shocked that she stopped, I felt like Dorothy in the 'Wizard of Oz' when the wicked witch dissolved into a puddle. Liberation surrounded me in waves.

As she was heading for the front door, Mother spoke like a petulant child, swearing that she was going to tell the neighbors what a hideous daughter I was. Gone for a few hours, she came back triumphant. Putting her arms in front of my face, she showed her badge of Victim Mother/Bad Daughter with her superficial scrapes, telling me that everyone now knew what a vicious, no-good daughter I was for scratching her.

It made an impact. From then on, Mother gave me a little distance. The red marks disappeared quickly, but the memory of the incident never did. Relief and amazement filled me. Though I did not want to find my power that way, it was the way it started.

COLLEGE

Choosing a college over 560 miles west, I took a plane and arrived in Cincinnati without knowing anyone. Quickly I made friends with the dorm students. The following day was orientation, when all the day students were there, too. So happy to connect, I made myself the greeter and reached out to everyone I could.

Soon students were divided up into academic groups, so there were many that I did not get to know well. Yet, I truly felt home with these students at this college for women, though I missed having men around.

Many of the college freshmen were homesick. Noticing I did not feel sad at all and they did, I thought I should call home eventually. There were no such things as cell phones. The one phone booth down the hall was share by 50 of us. The cost of a long distance call was a pocketful of quarters, depending on the length of the call. After a week, I called home. After that I knew I didn't need to call anymore. Those who were tearfully homesick, perplexed, and annoyed me.

CAR FOLLOW UP

During the midterm exams of the second semester of freshman year, winter was waning in Cincinnati. The snow was beginning to thaw and I was already looking forward to the end of the year. The summer break from the intense studying would feel freeing.

Pondering what to do when I headed home, I planned to get a summer job. However, I did not look forward to being around my mother even for short periods of time.

One saving grace was my beloved green Chevy that I had to leave at home. Dorm students were not allowed to have a car parked in the school lot through the year. Spaces were for the day students who drove to school and went home.

Though it had no power steering and drove like a Mack truck, in that last year of high school it took me everywhere I wanted to go. Everyone I knew rode with me.

Reminiscing in college about the joys of my car at home, I fantasized about my machine friend. I considered the places I would drive to in the coming summer, with whom I would go, and exactly when and why. In a feverish state, I wrote to my parents about my yearning for my car.

Dad was the only family member who communicated. I loved receiving his letters with his engineer printing that looked so neat and clear. Weeks later Dad responded to my message. Explaining that starting up my car once a week got tiresome, he told me that he sold my car. He sold it to his brother for my cousin, Judy, who was then a high school senior. To make it legal the sale included money - one whole dollar.

My car was gone. No one offered me the dollar either, though that may have exacerbated the pain.

It felt as if someone died. I felt the life drain out of me. A part of me felt dead. My ticket to autonomy was gone. I had bought the car with ALL my hard earned babysitting money that took three years to accumulate. Emptiness enveloped me.

Stunned and speechless, I justified my father's actions by thinking: "How stupid of me not to realize that the car would need starting. I really did not think of that. It was too much to expect that Dad would have to keep it going through the year while I was away. It seemed that the car, like me, took up space. It was too much trouble."

Yet, Dad had not mentioned that burden of the car's needs. At least, I had wanted to be consulted about what to do about it. I had no choice about leaving it at home if I wanted to go away to this college.

Still I figured Dad must be right. The sensible thing was that someone else could use it if it was too hard to maintain during the winter. "My desire to use it just for the summers was terribly selfish," I told myself. Yet, my dream of having it for the summers was crushed like pulverized glass.

The subject of my car did not come up again. No one considered that I might not be thrilled at the loss. Even Judy, the car recipient, never mentioned it.

Never did I see that green Chevy again and I never asked. It was like a good friend for whom I didn't get to say goodbye. Each summer, I felt very sad and limited having to take jobs that were either within walking distance, or on the bus line. Before I started teaching after college, the first thing I did was put a down payment on a car.

Since that Chevy was my first car, I did not realize that legally Dad could not sell my car without my signature since the car was in my name. My cousin Judy drove that car without an owner's license.

This experience underscored that my things did not count. Just as my clothes were given away at the orphanage, my beloved doll was damaged, my music records were broken, my statue was given away, my radio was threatened daily, the one-night Cinderella dress removed, and plenty of other examples. Then my car was sold without my consent. Or, was I a materialist? Was I too attached to things?

It occurred to me that these confiscated possessions that did not count to my loved ones, represented the fact that I did not matter to them. My mother, brothers, aunt, uncle, cousin and friends all knew that the car was given without my knowledge. No one indicated that anything was out of line. It appeared to be perfectly fine with everyone.

What I understood was that I had no rights. Always believing Dad was right in all he did, I had trouble speaking up for myself. The few times I did, I was derided by my dad. The past had taught me that my feelings were dismissed. Throughout my life I have had difficulty setting boundaries due to feeling I was not entitled to what was mine. I was not even entitled to my feelings.

FINDING KINDNESS FROM AN UNUSUAL SOURCE

Freshman year in college, I found food to be my friend. Breakfast and lunch was cafeteria style where the food was hot and delicious. The Russian cook, Mr. Popov, was always smiling and standing at attention now that his cooking work was finished and his staff was dishing out the food. Each student passed him in line. A short man, he was equally warm and friendly while being quiet and reticent. He appeared to be one who had been through a lot. Rumor had it that he was a refugee that owned a huge restaurant in Russia, having had to leave everything fast. The rumor made him all the more endearing to me.

Many students grumbled about the food. There was a rumor that the desserts had saltpeter in it to keep us from sexual desires. I didn't care. All ingredients tasted good to me. In this all female college, I was not tempted with out of control desires.

On one of these early college days, Mr. Popov saw me in line and whispered to me to see him before I left. Puzzled, I did what was requested. Surreptitiously, the cook brought me back to the kitchen area where students didn't go. He handed me a package, telling me to go to my room and eat the contents. Though my stomach was full, my eyes got big with the excitement of what could be in the box. It had to be a food package and it would be tasty coming from him. Even if there was a chance that I did not like the food, his thoughtfulness alone was a gift. Mr. Popov told me to tell no one. It was all for me. Thanking him profusely, I felt that this was better than gold.

Unable to fathom how I got so lucky, I walked back up the three flights of stairs feeling privileged. When I opened it, the box was filled with two-dozen huge chunky chocolate chip cookies, still warm from the oven. I recognized them from dessert. One of my four roommates was in the room and smelled the cookies. Keeping the box hidden in my desk, I shared a few with her, figuring I could eat the rest over the next week, or so.

Freshman year, dinner was a formal sit down each night. The big bowls of hot food on the table with a real white starched tablecloth was a treat. Never did I miss a meal. We were assigned tables and a professor, always a nun, sat with us. Quickly I got the reputation for finishing not just my plate, but also the bowls, if anything was left. Besides eating a lot, I loved talking, so I was often one of the last to leave the dinner hall.

At dinner, the meal had courses. First came the bread. It was in loaf form and it was not easy to cut since it was so light. Once we cut it and put it on our plates, it needed nothing. We could tear it easily still dripping with warm, moist, buttery taste. I was in heaven. For me that bread was a meal in itself.

At the dinner table, I was the human garbage

disposal. People would pass along the food without taking any; often grumbling about it so low that Sr. Margaret would not hear. Though I didn't think I liked vegetables, I would scoop them onto my plate, add mashed potatoes, and take meat like a ravenous animal.

Later, there was a cereal advertisement on TV about two brothers who didn't want to try a new cereal. They said: "Give it to Mickey." In college, I was Mickey. The only student who liked everything, I had no complaints.

The next day after lunch, Mr. Popov signaled me again to come to him. When I came to the kitchen, he gave me a whole loaf of luscious bread, wrapped in white paper. The butter from the bread was already coming through the paper. Mr. Popov made the best bread I ever tasted before or since.

Over the next nine months of school, Mr. Popov continued to give me food several times a week. It was food that could be wrapped easily and eaten without silverware. While honored to receive the bounty, I never knew for sure why Mr. Popov gifted me. Maybe it was because of the famished look I had, though I was not the only short and thin student.

There was no way any one person could eat all the muffins, cookies, breads, and cupcakes the cook gave me. So, much of the food I gave to others, and I appreciated every bit of it. It was a lesson in abundance, in sharing my unsought bounty. While I never told anyone my embarrassing home circumstances, at college I was very aware of having gone from near famine to enormous feast.

In my last year of high school I had gained fifteen pounds. That first year in college I gained an additional 15 pounds. When I got home that summer after freshman year, I weighed 105 and people said that I had "filled out at last."

That June, my parents came down to help me move out of the dorm. It was their only visit to that school building and the last year any students were in that building. It became a Motherhouse for the nuns.

Before leaving, I took my parents to meet someone special. It was not any of my professors, but rather Mr. Popov, who I knew would not be coming to the new building the next autumn. Sadly I said goodbye. I would not see him again.

A modern building opened in the fall, starting my sophomore year. Through the next three years in the new building, we students no longer had the same food service. It was a faceless corporation that ran it.

One advantage of the new system was that anyone had a chance to work in the kitchen for money. Since my father was slow in sending money, I needed to pay for books and supplies on my own. So I worked behind the scenes, witnessing first-hand that the new service was not about good ingredients or good taste. Lots of the food was right out of a can or a carton that you could buy at any grocery store.

Dinners were still formal, but the food was not even remotely comparable to what we had that first year. I still miss generous Mr. Popov, and not just for the food.

DRINKING

Dad prided himself on "holding his liquor." Though he drank heavily, Dad rarely appeared drunk. Yet, there were times when it was undeniable.

Drinking all Saturday, every Saturday, he would go to one or more of the local bars whenever he felt like it. Same drinking; different scenery. With his amazing capacity to hold liquor, he could keep drinking unnoticed. Only once did he appear to me to be inebriated. I figured he had his reasons.

The town drunk, our neighbor, Mr. Matthews, let the world know when he drank. Quite an introvert, Dad surprised us all that he got to know this neighbor. Until our neighbor moved after a few years, Dad and he hit the local bars often.

Mother worried that Mr. Matthews was a bad influence. A few times the two drinkers actually came up the street laughing. For Dad to be laughing, he had to be drunk. Dad seemed to be having a really good time. It was so incredibly rare that he enjoyed himself that I was amused and delighted for him. Usually, when he got to the house, no one could tell that he was drunk. He just looked happy. So good at faking, Dad could have worked for the CIA. Mr. Matthews made a fool of himself, but Dad was cucumber cool and arrow straight.

Definitely, Dad could hold his liquor and I could hold mine, too. I was just like him in masking the effects of drinking. Even more so, we both concealed the effects of our unwanted emotions.

In college, I called home one day and was told that Dad just got out of the hospital for hepatitis and jaundice.

"He just got out?" Knowing just enough health information, no one needed to tell me the cause. "Why didn't you tell me?" I quizzed. "Your Dad did not want you to worry," Mother explained.

I was surprised that Mother could keep the secret. Usually, she would not miss an opportunity to be the burdened victim of someone else's trouble. It may have been the long distance expense that kept her from calling. When I called, I was paying out of my cafeteria work paycheck. Even then, I was not told at the start of the call. Mother had other miscellaneous opinions to tell me first.

"What brought Dad to the doctor," I asked since Dad was not known for needing or seeking medical advice. "Doctor Andrews saw your father in church," Mother clarified.

"How did he know from looking?" I inquired. "Your father's skin was yellow, so Dr. Andrews told him to make an appointment."

When I came home that summer, I noticed that Dad had not quit drinking. Yet, his skin did not get yellow again. No one ever spoke of hepatitis thereafter. Neither hepatitis, nor alcohol, ever seemed to make any deleterious impact on his long-term health. When he died, he was just three months shy of his ninetieth birthday.

LIFE IS TENUOUS

My cousin, Judy, was injured in a car wreck in her last year of college. It was not the car that once was mine. She was in the backseat of her friend's Volkswagen celebrating the completion of her graduate degree in hematology. In shock, I was moved to visit her in the Philadelphia Hospital on the first weekend. It was dreadful. She could not move her arms or legs. In fact, she was a paraplegic, confined to a bed.

Deeply saddened, I thought of this once spirited and healthy young lady deprived of moving around. It was next to the worst nightmare I could imagine. The worst would be having mental illness like my mother.

The time was just after I had moved to New Jersey, where I taught reading to middle school children. On Saturdays, I made the 90-minute drive to spend the day with Judy and her parents.

Judy's mother was the embodiment of doom and gloom. It was hard to be there. Anything was difficult to talk about in this family, since they were present to nothing but loss. Who could blame them? I did not talk about my life since it was in stark contrast to Judy's. No one inquired since they did not want to hear it. I could not talk about movies or books, since my uncle and aunt were absorbed in the immediate needs of Judy's bodily fluids, the rate of absorption of the various IVs, the complications of the injuries, and the surgeries to come. Her devastated parents told of their sleep deprivation, their deep fears, and their bleak future with their dependent offspring.

Comforting words from me would sound hollow. Such thoughts would mock the present reality. While usually talkative, I felt awkward, useless, and restrained. I felt almost guilty for being mobile. Always the one whose health was questionable, I felt survivor's guilt, even though I wasn't at the accident.

Even doctors doubted that I would make it to adulthood. Seeing my cousin so injured turned the world upside down. It made no sense. Obviously, Judy's condition wasn't the way it was supposed to be.

Only after a long day with my cousin and her parents, did I feel it was acceptable to leave. Walking away, I felt tears flowing for the meaninglessness of it all.

Judy, up until the moment before the accident, had a bright future in the medical field. With her boyfriend, she was planning a wedding and family. None of it looked possible now. Bitterly, her mother made it clear. Her only child would have no children, no life worth living. Judy's parents would be burdened with her care for the rest of their lives.

YELLOW PAGES

"Home is where the heart is." Ever since leaving home I have loved that quote. Actually everyone knew that was my signature quote. I made signs with those words, gluing them on top of cardstock that I covered with colorful wrapping paper. I gave them to my friends.

Saving quotes ever since I worked on my high school newspaper, I collected hundreds and yet this was my preferred one. It was ironic that I had to go away to find my heart. My home, I realized, was within me.

All my college peers were excited to finish this first year. I was thrilled to see the temporary end of the constant pressure of exams and the continuous demands of professors. I loved the thought of getting away. Yet, get away to what? I had little to look forward to and a lot to dread.

Just after my eighteenth birthday, I had completed my first semester and went home for Christmas, hundreds of miles and a twelve-hour Greyhound Bus ride from the house where I grew up.

Returning to my childhood house felt strange. Each family member seemed even more disassociated and disengaged. We seemed like people from separate worlds who just happened to be under the same roof for many years. It was that way before I left. Now it was more obvious. Maybe I should not have come back.

There were no friends staying at the college over the two-week holiday break, so I came home out of not knowing what to do with myself. I dreaded being back, yet I wanted to see Barb and other friends. Outside of a brief time with friends, it was not a happy time overall. Friends were starting families and busy with their relatively new life.

Then at the end of the college year, I was back in PA for the summer, working as a store clerk and cashier at a new toy and furniture store for children. Walking home on lunch break, I came into the disheveled house where I lived. If a burglar ever came and ransacked the place, no one could tell the difference. If that burglar tried to steal anything, he would have left disappointed, unable to find anything of value.

That noontime, the house looked even worse than when I left only hours ago. It was hard to believe that Mother could make it worse.

No matter, I was here for a quick bite. Relieved that Mother wasn't home, I scrounged around, looking for something edible. In an attempt to repay some of my college expenses, I always gave my parents the bulk of my paycheck, except for $3 a week; therefore I could not afford to eat out. I wouldn't have thought of it, if I could have afforded that luxury. At the store, there was no refrigerator for staff to keep a sandwich, so I had to go home to eat.

A muffled sound came to my consciousness. Recognizing the telephone sound, I looked around. Finding the ringing phone was a challenge. Even the cord was hidden, so I had to follow the sound that was hardly audible. Finally I found the cord, but as usual that was the first of a series of challenges to overcome.

The cord was not laid out in a straight line. It required lifting layers of things such as newspapers on top of a phonebook, which was on top of Mother's bathrobe next to a box of mixed things, some old books, broken knickknacks and several heavy items. Just as I found the first few feet of the cord, it wrapped around another direction underneath yet more items.

It would seem that just pulling the cord was the answer, but that would break the cord. The piles were heavy, thick and unwieldy. After coming across at least 60 odd pieces of trash, the sound continued so I kept working. The sound stopped; then started up again right away.

Whoever was on the line really was determined to make this connection. At last, after spanning two rooms I found the end of the cord where the phone sat upside down.

As I answered it, a man's voice with an edge told me that my mother was a public nuisance. Wow," I thought: "Word really spread." He went on to tell me that he would have to call the police if someone did not come and get her immediately. He was the administrator of the local hospital.

Mother had been walking the halls annoying people who were trying to get well, he explained. Oh boy, I could sympathize. I was tempted to tell him that she could do more than annoy sick people. Mother had the power to make healthy folk sick, too. But he was already in no mood.

While I told the administrator that I had to go back to work, he gave me no choice. He said that if no one came within the hour, he would call authorities.

Dad, I knew, would not forgive me for letting police get involved. Also, my father would be angry if I called his work and asked him to pick up his wife. His job was more important than mine. Jerry was away in the army. Not knowing the whereabouts of my 15 year-old brother, I was the only one.

Calling into work, I apologized saying I had a family emergency. I felt for my co-workers who could not go to lunch until I got back.

Hercules wouldn't want this task that was in front of me. The administrator told me where he had detained my mother. I knew it was not easy to keep her contained. He must have known that she was not mentally well, yet he gave no hint as he described where his office was. I considered telling him that he should put her on the sixth floor, the psychiatric ward. Mother had been there before in the psychiatric ward. It would be a perfect solution.

Then I thought better of my possible suggestion. Evidently, the sixth floor ward was not for hardcore cases. It was my hunch that the hospital could not handle her, and did not want her again. It was probably why Dad sent her to a more expensive place the last time. Besides, Dad would say that I had no right to imply my mother was mentally ill, because she was just fine. Annoying people was classic behavior for her. Nothing out of the ordinary.

Since my car belonged to my cousin, I had to pick up Mother by bus, wait for another bus, get her on and off both buses, walk her home, and run back to work. How I hated buses.

The first part of the trip, I waited in the hot sun not far from where I worked. That was tense. "What if someone sees me?" I stressed. In our little valley, buses were notoriously off schedule all the time. The two bus rides back were no fun either.

Belligerent Mother, offended by the administrator, ranted about that mean man who was too damn dumb to understand her generosity in 'entertaining the sick.' That was one of the Ten Commandments, she insisted. She justified her position to each member of the captured audiences on both buses.

Running back to work, I was terribly out of breath. Making up some wild story to explain my lateness, I knew the truth would have seemed a lot crazier and a lot less credible to the uninitiated in such matters. No coworker or boss knew my home situation. I wanted to keep it that way, despite how unhappy they were about this infraction of the rules. Inconveniencing them brought me deep distress.

When Dad came home I followed him into the bedroom when Mother wasn't in there. In the midst of cluttered chaos, I told him what happened that day. He was unmoved and undaunted. Explaining that it was unsafe for the neighborhood to leave Mother alone, I talked to him a long time and insisted: "Mother's behavior indicates that it is time to do something." Since Dad replied that he didn't know what to do, I found the Yellow Pages, one of the things I discovered under the pile of junk while looking for the phone. I told Dad to look under P for psychiatrist; or else I would. He took the phonebook and leafed through it, looking depressed and uneasy. I left him alone with his mission. He didn't communicate after that.

Never did I think to acknowledge to my father, or to myself, that Mother's illness was hurting her family members. Knowing all the while I grew up that my friends had organized homes and stable mothers, I still couldn't grasp that I might have a right to a normal life. That was unthinkable at the time.

A decade earlier, it was clear that Mother's sister Eleanor was upset by Mother's lack of housekeeping skills. Aunt Eleanor came over one whole day and organized things with Mother's permission. But Mother made a point to undo Eleanor's work before she left. Eleanor was visibly upset and my mother retaliated verbally against her sister. Aunt Eleanor's husband called to say she wouldn't be coming over again. My father said that was fine. So no problem, right?

Dad regularly preached the gospel that we had a good life and that others were messed up. He didn't flinch at the regular tirades and the daily disrespect, unless Mother directed it at him. His tolerance was unlimited when directed at others.

The next day Dad was still home when I walked to work. He was helping Mother find clothes to put on. She often didn't wear regular clothes, even on a good day for her. So, I knew this was the day. He must be taking her to the psychiatrist.

We didn't speak, and we both knew. I was hungry for more information, but dared not question.

At work I skipped lunch and stayed late to make up for some of the time I missed the day before. When I got home Dad was there, but not Mother. He explained that when he told the doctor the symptoms, the doctor recommended Mother go straight to a state hospital. It was an awful feeling. I was glad that I missed her being taken away this time.

Immediately, I started fixing dinner with the little that I could find around. Though Dad said nothing, I fantasized that he was grateful.

After that, every moment I had, I cleaned up the disarray. Worn out from work and worry, Dad did not participate. It took three weeks to get the house somewhat functional.

Then Mother came home more hostile than usual. It made me wonder what good it was to have her go to the hospital. The hospital system made money but the result was that Mother was usually worse. I could not see any improvement.

Before the first day ended, the house was in shambles again. That made her comfortable. Meanwhile, I could relate to Sisyphus rolling that stone endlessly uphill.

CHURCH ANNOUNCEMENT

While I was teaching, I visited home on occasion. One evening I stayed overnight in the room in which I grew up. My concern was about offending my parents if I came to visit my hospitalized cousin and not them. Like my aunts and uncles, my parents did not inquire about my teaching job, my friends, my coworkers, my boss, or even my apartment.

On Sunday, I went to church alone. My parents attended an earlier Mass. My brothers weren't sure when they were going. There were about eight Masses to choose.

Entering the vestibule, I saw a fellow I knew from high school. Jim had been in my homeroom all four years. Just after graduation he indicated he was interested in having a close relationship with me. I did not think he even noticed me all those years. Jim had said that he thought very highly of me. I hadn't stayed around town long enough to find out how high.

At the time Jim first reached out to me, I could not grasp a long distance relationship. Now that I was living closer to our hometown, maybe it wasn't too late for possible romance. He smiled brightly in recognition. Then he moved to a pew and joined a pretty woman with a baby. Seeing him then with his beautiful family, I was happy for him.

Sitting in the straight back, hard, church seat, it reminded me of the prevailing philosophy that life is uncomfortable and rigid, too. Who was I to disagree with that?

Looking around I saw several more high school chums, some that I knew even in grade school. We exchanged discreet waves of recognition. It really was good to be back where I knew folks from the past, people who did not disappear from this place, as I had done.

Just then Mass was starting. For announcements, the priest came to the podium regally, yet his voice droned on, like a very bad actor in a B movie. I saw no value in attending Mass, but it took less time and trouble than it would take to argue with my parents about not going. My philosophy of an ideal church consisted of people sharing what was important to them, making room for the wisdom inside them to emerge. I wanted to talk with these people that I knew and loved.

Ironically, always when Mass ended, people raced out the door to their cars where they waited in line to get away from the church. Attending Mass was required for Catholics. When something is not voluntary, the purpose is often lost.

It was time for prayer announcements. Always I dreaded this part, hearing about others' troubles. Since I prayed for the whole town, I figured that I didn't need every dreary detail.

The priest appealed for prayers for Judy, my dear cousin who was in the hospital as a paraplegic. I was glad that others would pray. In the next breath, the priest asked the congregation to pray for me, who was also seriously ill. He said my name. Everyone heard.

Seriously ill? Oh my God. I was on fire. My face must have reflected the alarm I felt. Wanting to run out of there to hide my shame and embarrassment, I knew that would bring additional attention to me. More than half the people in that church knew my identity, and they could see that I was fine. What must they think of me? Would they think I wanted to compete with my cousin's health challenge?

What a shock. Yet in an instant, I knew who did this. My mother did not want her sister-in-law, Judy's mother, to get more sympathy than Mother did.

Announcements were the same in all the Masses, so both my parents heard this already. Dad made no mention of this equating Judy's intense, life and death needs with my physical problems that were ignored in our home. I felt nauseous through the rest of the long Mass. I did not go to communion.

It was a big church so I moved quickly before my former classmates could get near me. I became like one that I judged, one that avoided peers and avoided speaking. Plowing through the throng, I made no eye contact. Heading straight to my car, I vowed never to go back to this church. Even so, I reminded myself that I could not afford to care about what anyone thought. I must keep moving on.

After my brothers came back from church, I scanned their faces for any sign of their having heard the announcements. Evidently, they thought nothing of it. While I was livid, I said nothing.

JUDY

Years later with great exertion, extraordinary effort, and abundant rehabilitation, Judy managed to get enough movement in her hands to type. Since her degree was in hematology, she wrote several medical books on the subject, based on her direct experiences with blood work. Her sweet, sunny disposition made others delight in her aliveness. Her parents worked hard to make her life feasible at home. It took her parents, nurses, and others working round the clock every day to keep her sustained.

Besides writing books, Judy used as much of what she had available in her life to stay lively and connected. Through e-mail she kept in touch with her many far-flung cousins. Her love for others never dimmed. She brought some of us together who didn't know each other. For her, I remain very thankful.

At age 55, 33 years after the car accident, she died following an operation necessitated by complications from her injury. While her body was limited, her spirit was inspirational.

NO ESCAPE FROM MOTHER

After doing social work in Oklahoma, I took a high school teaching job in Pennsylvania. Having been far away for a full year, I got strong enough to disallow my mother's uncontainable anger to attack me. For once in my life, my father, in the first ever acknowledgment of reality, suggested that it was best to avoid giving Mother my new phone number.

My apartment was about 15 miles from my parents' home. Dad knew the new number, but intended to keep it from Mother. He promised to relay messages between us. His support was a one-of-a-kind recognition of my mother's hostility and viciousness toward me.

Just two days later, my mother called the high school where I was teaching. Just before school let out that day, the school principal called me over the loudspeaker the same way students are called when they are in trouble.

Until then, Fr. Murphy appeared as an aging 50-something Santa in a cassock. As principal, he had a private office. That was where I first met with him when he told me that I was highly qualified for the position as English Teacher for 9th, 10th and 11th grade students.

This time however, he required that I meet him in the hub, the main office where secretaries worked and dozens of teachers and students walked through at any given time.

Obviously, I thought his message must be impersonal, since it was such a public place. His usual friendly smile was replaced with something ominous. He looked at me like I was a criminal. Heatedly, he informed me publicly that my mother was broken hearted that I refused to tell her where I lived, or how to contact me.

"Hmm," I thought, "obviously she figured out how to contact me. Broken-hearted? Nothing could be further from the truth. Maybe broken-hearted that she couldn't abuse me," I continued musing in my head.

At least 30 people were in the big office. They stood frozen in shock, like live statues wondering what my move would be as the priest continued scolding me, describing the worst daughter in the history of the known world. "How could you deprive your mother? How could you do this? Do you realize how you hurt your poor mother..." he berated me with his words, delivery and tone.

No one who accidentally stumbled in that main office wanted to interrupt or disturb this drama. It was clear that the Good Father had made up his mind as he deliberately punished me in front of students, secretaries and teachers. He decided he was judge, jury and jailer with his instant assessment. Up until that point, he had respected me for the job I had been doing.

More students were crowding in, stopping as they were bumping into the statues already in place. When the booming words stopped, I was the center of people's stares. Everyone wanted to hear my response ... especially me. So bombarded, my mind was overwhelmed.

Even the sound of footsteps stopped outside the glass wall of the main office where more people heard and gathered in the main hallway. I was surrounded inside and outside the office and from all sides. The air was as still as the silence. I had better make this good. What rabbit could I pull out of this hat? Who would or could ever see my point? What chance did I have?

Not for a moment did I look away. I kept my gaze on the red, round Irish face of this priest. He scowled, waiting for an explanation. I quickly assessed my options.

With his attitude, there was no possibility of redemption for me. I had been condemned without a trial. His handling of this as a confrontation indicated that nothing I could say would change his mind. This was not the place for me to defend myself or to share about my mother's history.

Finally I spoke. Simply I said: "Thank you" as if it had been a pleasant message that I just heard. Then I turned on my high heels immediately, looking forward. Outwardly undisturbed, I passed the stunned students who heard it all out in the hall.

While I deeply resented the principal for his assumption, I knew how skilled my mother was at ensnaring innocent people into her traps. I fumed at the thought of my mother, ever the Master Manipulator. Not wanting to give her the satisfaction, I never mentioned the incident to her. I never enlightened Fr. Murphy either. At the end of that school year, I handed in my resignation, not knowing where I would work next.

AFTER SCHOOL

As a high school teacher, I socialized after school on Fridays with other teachers. Since my apartment was very near the high school where I taught, everyone came to my place. Greeting each one warmly, I would inquire, "What can I get you to drink?"

One particular Friday, I would have preferred to just go to sleep. Having a very bad cold, I told my co-workers not to get close to me since my cold was getting worse and I hardly got through the day.

My words weren't enough. Coming through the door with a bottle, Jack joked: "Just add some orange juice to this vodka." He winked at me with his charming good looks. "Oh, the vitamin C will save me," I shot back laughingly. "I like that."

No one else minded that I was losing my voice. They did not know that a cold quickly could turn into pneumonia for me. I considered myself lucky that the school system in PA did not require a physical, though the NJ school system harassed me all through the year about that and I never complied. Dealing with my physical reality was too uncomfortable. I did see a general practitioner weekly for allergy shots, and that was all. On this afternoon I told myself everything was all right. I was fine. I could handle whatever came. I always did.

Having company invariably made me feel upbeat. That was healthy, I figured. I brushed off the signals that my body was sending, including the throat lined with sandpaper. Knowing that I needed to get groceries by the next day, I wished that I had something nutritious to eat or drink with all this liquor.

Typically, on Friday after school, we never got into eating. No one expected food. I rarely had anything to eat for myself much less anyone else. So I continued to drink with my co-workers. For hours we discussed, debated, and laughed.

When my friends left, I left everything as it was and went straight to bed. Upon waking, the clock said it was an hour earlier than when I fell asleep. Yet, it was dark just as it had been when I last saw the clock. How could this be? Could eleven hours have gone by? It was 5 AM. My head was hot. My mind was foggy. I fell asleep again.

When I awoke the second time it was late afternoon. Reaching for the phone next to my bed, I pulled it to me and started dialing. While I went to a doctor for allergy shots, I could not remember that doctor's number. While frustrated, I couldn't stay awake.

Dawn was coming up. It must be Sunday, having missed Saturday altogether. I knew that I had to call somebody. Should I call Amy? She may not be up yet.

Next time I awoke it was high noon. The phone was making noise off the hook. I must not have completed dialing before falling asleep again. This time, I was determined to stay awake long enough to finish dialing 7 numbers. How hard could this be? It took enormous effort. I had to dial fast, but this circular dial was hard work as it moved in slow motion. The one number I could recall was my parents' number. I started moving that dial with all my heart.

Success.

My parents heard the weak sound of my voice and promised that they would come over with food. Fortunately, my father had a copy of my apartment key. As I fell back to sleep, I remembered that the living room was probably a sight to behold, but I could do nothing about it.

On arriving, my parents found my living room strewn with half-empty bottles of rye, bourbon, rum, and vodka. My kitchen cabinets had whiskey as a staple at all times. You would not find flour or pasta there. In the fridge, you would find no butter or eggs, and rarely milk. I didn't see the need.

Breakfast consisted only of a flavored orange powdered drink mixed with water. It had some Vitamin C in it, though way too much sugar. Lunch was provided at the school. Dinner, well I skipped that most days. Eating took energy for me. When I couldn't breathe, I couldn't eat.

Coming into my bedroom after seeing my place, my father looked as sick as I was. I assured him that I didn't drink all that. Not amused, he looked at me as one would look at a mangy stray dog. I comforted myself with the knowledge that it was not the alcohol consumption that put me in this condition. Still, I realized it did not help to drink when I needed nutrition and sleep. I never could turn down a party, especially when it was mine.

My parents told me that it was Sunday night. They took me to their home since I was not likely to recover for several days. My biggest regret was in knowing that I would miss a day of teaching and I'd have to see a doctor to verify my illness if I missed more than that.

Though grateful for my parents' help, I knew that the dusty, mold-infested bedroom where I grew up would impede any healing. I dreaded my mother's attention-getting intrusions. Yet, on this occasion, Mother did not get in the way. For the most part, she let me sleep and brought me food. Maybe she saw something that scared her. My breathing problems never did.

Now that my mother knew where I lived, she never wrote. By that time, she could have found out my phone number, and never called. It was fine with me.

Fortunately, I never became addicted to alcohol. I was addicted to people. I stopped drinking regularly when I married Ed, a non-drinker. Always a social activity for me, it wasn't any fun drinking alone.

ONE VISIT

My husband Ed's orientation to life was that an offspring needed to honor their parents. The way to do that was to visit. I felt guilty that I did not want to. Our daughter was four and my parents had not seen her in a year. Ed thought we should make the twelve-hour drive from Cincinnati to Philadelphia.

Reluctantly, I agreed, though my parents did not say they wanted a visit. We booked a place to stay. When the day came, Ed had the luggage and the car packed efficiently. He put our four year-old daughter in a car seat and waited for me. I sat on the couch trying to breathe well enough to walk the short distance to the car. Ed came back to see what was the matter. I had to lean on him all the way out to the car. For me, it was excruciatingly difficult to breathe, and more so than usual that day. It was also agonizingly difficult to visit my parents. I blamed my body for letting me down again. Conflicted, I knew that if we didn't leave soon, we wouldn't get there in time to visit my folks that night before we went to the hotel.

When we got to their house, we thought my parents would be happy to see their granddaughter. I had no expectation they'd be happy to see my husband or me, not for any particular reason other than they never showed much interest in us.

My parents continued to watch TV in the dark. When one show went off, they watched another randomly. It was exactly as if we were not there. Even their granddaughter was a non-event. It was not personal. Jerry lived alone in the same house with our parents. He did not eat meals with them and rarely spoke as he walked through the house to get what he needed. No one was upset with anyone else. That is just what they did.

Though I knew Jerry must have heard us come in, I knew I'd have to go to his bedroom to see him. He would have gone to sleep rather than coming out to greet me. Knocking on his bedroom door, I waited until he opened it at his leisure. As he unbolted his door, I noticed that indifference to life permeated his small room that remained unchanged in the decade since he shared it with our brother.

Asking how things were going for him at work, he answered in a sound that was left up to me to interpret. It was caveman-speak from him.

Whenever I called to talk to Jerry, it was the same grunt for an answer. It was the best I could get since he never initiated a conversation, or a phone call. "Come on, tell me what's going on in your life." To break the awkward silence, I tried another approach: "How are our parents doing, really?" Nothing came out. I figured he didn't want to think about anything, much less talk about anything, whether real or superficial.

"I'm here for you whenever you want to talk," I said as I left his cold room and empty silence.

COMMUNICATION

After moving to SW Ohio from NY, I continued calling my parents regularly at least every two weeks. It wasn't something I looked forward to.

It was my mother who got on the phone. Dad didn't talk much and Jerry almost never got on the phone unless Mother harassed him. Mother talked *to* me, not with me. Her monologues were endless, overlapping stories of her past with numerous people from various decades. Nothing had changed since I was a little girl listening to Mother talk about herself. It was less a stream of consciousness than a stagnant, putrid pond. Trying to make sense of the jumbled story, I would show genuine interest by asking questions to sort out who was who. A question would provoke her anger, as she accused me of not following her illogical run-on sentences.

When mother and I were on the phone, it was her monologue, hodgepodge of stories from her past. She was always the star heroine. In those calls, I was so occupied by the black cloud that was there and fending off the mindless chatter that I did not notice what was missing.

Real connection was absent. Even though I called her usually, I felt annoyed being a captured audience to her rambling, and I accepted that it was the best I could get. So distracted was I by avoiding and resisting the black hole that was ready to swallow me whole, I just endured a barrage of endless criticism.

When I discovered that anytime I said: "Just a minute I'll be right back," she would keep going as if I didn't say anything. So I learned to make uh-huh sounds for the first five minutes, and then put the phone down for an hour or more. Mother entertained herself, continued to talk, unconcerned that there was no response. For both our sakes, I gave up engaging. Her monologues could last for hours. After awhile I'd check back and tell her someone was at the door and I had to hang up now. That way I did not hear as many stories. No questions, no confusion. We were both better off.

For some years, Mother would start off informing me about Colleen, as if Colleen had been my friend. Mother would never tell me about the people who were my friends. Knowing that I had not seen Colleen since high school decades earlier, Mother would visit Colleen regularly and interact with her eight children as if they were her own grandchildren. Rarely would Mother ask about my daughter and almost never remembered Ilona's birthday. But Mother obsessed in stories about Colleen's children, and their birthday parties to which she invited herself. I was surprised Colleen tolerated my mother. She must have been very lonely.

To Mother, Colleen was acceptable because she had a lots of children and a turbulent life. Giving Colleen unsought opinions on child rearing, on smoking cessation, and other topics, Mother got to be in charge. Gleefully for hours, she would talk about everything about Colleen's life, her volatile marital relationship, her kids illnesses, her neighbors, relatives, and on and on. It was a soap opera. Not interested in soaps or sad lives, I walked away from the phone.

My sympathies went out to Colleen. She became one of the ones that dealt with Mother in person. Clearly I realized that my peaceful life was boring to my mother. Disappointed that I did not offer shocking news and dramatic fireworks, Mother sought new sources of excitement in people I once knew.

Eventually after many years, Mother stopped talking about Colleen. I never asked. Colleen must have put a stop to Mother's intrusions. Who could blame her?

Rarely did Mother ask anything about my life. When I told her something, she didn't listen. The two things she did know about me, she did not like. These things were fodder for her rage.

The main two accusations Mother had for her endless criticism were that I did not have enough children and I was a 'fallen away Catholic.' With that, she could find nothing good in me and felt it was her job to let me know. Often, she assured me she was trying to save my soul.

Mother thought that I did not have a real family because I had only one child. The fact that it took Herculean physical effort for me to keep up with one child, had no bearing on her demands.

Secondly, I left the religion I was raised in. I defied the premise: "Once a Catholic, always a Catholic." Probably the real issue was that, to my parents, leaving their religion was equal to leaving *them*. I had broken away from the tribe, the source of everything sacred.

It was not that my life was all "sunshine, lollipops and roses." Of course, there were sorrows that I could have told my parents about my life. I knew there could be no safety, and no comfort in sharing.

Once, my father asked how I was and I told him that I had just recovered from pneumonia after being in a hospital for a week. Dad told me it happened because I had left the church, studied comparative religions, and worked at a Unity Church. Too resigned to speak, I didn't point out the multiple times I was in a hospital for pneumonia while I was Catholic.

Just to start something, Mother would call only on Sundays. That way she could 'ask' if I went to Mass that day. Patiently, I would tell her she knew the answer. Furthermore, I'd affirm that God was big enough to love me anyway.

Dad didn't say much, though he found me objectionable, too. I had failed to please, as I was. My choices worked for me, but not for my parents. They would have preferred that I please them rather than travel my authentic path. Their unhappiness with me was sad, but being someone I wasn't would have been tragic. For me, there was no winning with them.

There were times I felt driven to connect with Mother. Wanting to have one meaningful conversation, I eventually despaired of that ever happening.

One day, I realized that possibly the reason my mother never stopped criticizing was because I never acknowledged that I heard her. I assumed that she hated me and was treating me with loathing to match her feeling. On this one day, I decided to give my mother the benefit of the doubt. Maybe there was a rational part of her. What was my part in this?

Could she have felt that I was not taking her seriously? Absolutely. My perennial resistance to hearing the disapproving things she said must have contributed to her repeating the negative messages. Knowing the difference between acknowledging and agreeing, I wrote to her. I acknowledged that I understood her messages, her disappointments, her upsets. Without emotion or apology, I gave recognition to her specific discontent with me. I wrote that I heard it without admission of right or wrong.

Immediately, Mother wrote back on a postcard, communicating that I was O.K. and that she loved me. That was a miracle. It was the first ... and the last time she said I was O.K.

The next time I heard from her, the same criticism was there as though nothing changed. Still, on some level, something was different for me. I knew there was some remote part of her that loved me, even if it was temporary and fleeting. Even my mother had more than one dimension. The loving part was hidden and inaccessible. But it was there, somewhere. Just knowing that, gave me strength. It cracked the concrete that my mother was to me. It reminded me that I loved her, too.

PARTING THOUGHTS

After living with my parents, I realized that I had a life force underneath that concrete slab of obstacles, just as the common, unappreciated weed seeks the light, and comes forth, no matter what is in the way. That is the kind of life force possible in all of us. With it came the dream that I could get to the other side.

Somewhere inside the dismal times, I imagined there was a way out, though I could not specifically picture it. It was a long while before I thought I could have anything good come true.

When in the middle of it, it was not easy to see. Yet I discovered that everything could contribute to me, if I let it. The gift is in taking what is there and using it to grow spiritual strength.

Soon, I began to realize that good things did come to me. My husband and daughter loved me. I had loving friends and co-workers. This occurred all the while I was rejecting myself. I couldn't see that I was making my life work, despite my self-doubts.

Like the wild flower that breaks through a sidewalk, love can grow through the concrete of pain. Somewhere under the tangible obstacles that block one's way, love is the unstoppable life force that can smash through. Without the concrete, the flower could not grow as strongly, or as victoriously.

It's a good thing that no one told the weed or flower that it was impossible. The flower would have thought itself too weak, too fragile, or too ugly to accomplish any such feat. It just does what is natural to it.

We listen to the messages that are around us, in our environment. If we haven't been told from external sources that we can't, we hear it internally. The voice in our head tells us we are not enough. When we believe it, we are victims of our mind even more than victims of circumstance. The healthy voice in our head says that there has to be a break in this concrete somewhere.

Throughout life, I looked for opportunities to express and grow just as the flower finds a break somewhere in the concrete, an opening that can be expanded enough to reach freedom.

Stepping out in leadership and achieving outer success in teaching and writing, I traveled a whole summer in Europe alone, married husband Ed, experienced giving birth, and raised my child. While mothering my lively daughter, I worked as a reading teacher, later as a youth director and now a relationship coach.

At the same time I compensated for what I did not receive early in life. Since I knew some physical hunger as a child, I became a volunteer Community Leader of The Hunger Project, an international organization. Since I understood emotional conflict and neglect, I volunteered as a mentor to several local children in the International Youth At Risk Program.

While moving ahead, I experienced pulmonary setbacks that landed me several times in emergency rooms. Later, just as Ed nurtured me through illnesses, I supported him through surgery and months of cancer treatments.

My childhood affected my automatic response to others. Hearing hysterics from my mother, I did not recognize my husband's anger outbursts as depression, since it was so enmeshed in my childhood.

After 23 years of marriage when Ed refused to get help for life-long depression, I recognized that my tolerance for his moods was not helping him, and it was hurting me. Our daughter was grown.

Appreciating that my life had value to me was another level of freedom. It cost me the dream of the continuous marriage that I desired. Having done everything possible to make our marriage work, I had erroneously thought I could make it work even if Ed didn't. After holding myself 100% responsible all those years, my one hundred percent was not enough to keep us together.

At middle age, I quit a 12-year employment as youth director. The next day, I recognized I needed to leave my husband as well. I knew that I needed to support me.

Separating from Ed cost me some friends who would not accept me as a single woman. Moving into a small apartment, I relied on my ability to make a viable salary to pay my bills. It was the best thing I could have done for both of us. While living in separate places, Ed and I remained good friends. There is more on this period of time in the Amazon best seller *Overcomers Inc.,* an anthology in which I contributed the chapter: *The Weed That Grew Out of the Sidewalk.*

No longer attached to making our marriage work, I spoke more authentically. That allowed Ed to reveal his unspoken thoughts. That opened a world for us to explore. We understood what did not work and created new ways to support each other.

After medical help, Ed got depression under control. We exchanged vows to love and live together again. Barb, who had been my Matron of Honor and her husband Joe, who had been Best Man, came to a ceremony on a beach to honor the new vows Ed and I created together. Those vows meant even more this second time around.

This renewed marriage has lasted since 1997. Fulfillment and satisfaction permeate our lives in a way that neither of us could have imagined. Through a five year separation, the two of us arrived at the deep mutual connection we have now. We continue to thrive.

Everyone has experienced the sting of life's bite at some time. My message is that wherever you feel trapped, there is always some choice. Furthermore out of the darkness of chaos, the challenges look concrete solid. It is by pushing beyond the concrete that the light can come through. Then, joy can be birthed.

Rather than condemn your past, you can revisit what you remember and see what good could come from it.

What you think of the past is what shapes you. How did your past contribute to your present strength? What are your current strong points? What are your gifts, not just in terms of qualities, but also in your state of joy, love, and peace? These are some questions I use in my coaching practice for each one desiring a good relationship to self.

From an airplane you can see the sun even if the rain is falling on the ground below. Similarly, by moving above a challenge, you can shift from pain to peace. A life of struggle and turmoil can evolve into a life of delight and wholeness. I honor you, dear reader, for I know you have done that plenty of times in your life.

Challenges can be altered by what we make of it. How we view those circumstances makes all the difference. Despite the fact that I had very little power to direct my life as a child, and certainly responded in childish ways, I made choices to direct my life away from the pain. Rather than see myself as a victim, I see myself as an overcomer. Rather than a survivor, I see myself as a thriver who daily practices jumping over physical, mental and emotional hurdles.

In childhood, I did not consciously choose those obstacles. In adulthood, whenever aware, I can continually choose how I see things, people and circumstances. When aware, I can choose how I feel about them. Like everyone else, I am not always aware.

The past affects us in one way, or another. The difference is in what we say about it. What is the story you tell about your life? Does that story lift you, or deflate you? I invite you to see how you overcame your past and how you triumphed over circumstances.

Mother died two years after Dad, when she was 90. She had more episodes in mental institutions, even after Dad died. Her last mental hospital experience was three weeks before her death.

When I called her, she told me that she did not like the people at the mental institution. Triumphantly, Mother described how she showed them her attitude: " I banged my cane against the walls in the middle of the night."
"What did you do when nurses took your cane away?" I inquired.
"I have my ways," she whispered.

The next day Mother had another story. "I banged my shoes on the walls last night." "Well, did they let you keep your shoes?" "They can't stop me," she said prophetically. The next day, her newest device was unveiled. "Last night I banged my fists on the walls." While visualizing Mother being tied up as the next step, and wasn't sure that was still done.
"Is it worth it?" I wondered out loud.
"I DON'T LIKE THEM," Mother insisted as if I had not been listening. In her world, I still was not supposed to have a different opinion.

In her way, Mother went out of this life basically kicking and screaming, not only in resistance, but also in protest. While in that mental ward, she caught pneumonia. Then she was moved to a cardiac floor where she went into a coma and died shortly after.

It is hard to grieve the loss of a mother when she is there threatening you every day. There were times as an adult when in agony of breathing problems were so bad that I found myself moaning the word *Mom.* I was shocked at myself. The sound was a betrayal of my grown-up persona, the one that did not identify with a mother.

Momentarily I wondered if I meant the woman who birthed me. Then, I figured I was calling out an archetypal mother, one I never had. I found this curious. Maybe the word "mom" was a simple guttural sound that signaled the little energy I had when air was in short supply in my lungs. Even though I didn't want to admit it, I had longing.

In my forties, I sat in a theater with my daughter watching *Little Orphan Annie* singing the song: *Tomorrow.* Feeling annoyed with the orphan on the screen, I had the thought: "Give me a break. That child could not be so naive as to think her mother was coming for her." With the force of a cement truck running over me, I realized that I harbored the deep desire that my mother would come for me, that she would love me, that she would acknowledge my worth. My mother would get well!

After far more decades than Little Orphan Annie had, I still held hidden hope that I'd connect meaningfully with Mother. "How could I be so pitifully dumb?," I wondered.

How did I hide that need from myself? Immediately, I wanted to give up the illusion of *someday.*

It was hope that led me a year earlier to present Dad with the good news that the bi-polar and schizophrenia psychiatrist Dr. E. Fuller Torrey, was practicing in a nearby state. Dr. Torrey was the best hope. We could do this.

Dad wanted no part of Mother getting such expert help. Offering no reason, he was adamant against any attempt at getting any real help.

Stunned at his response, I sorrowfully suspected that Dad feared if his wife changed, he would have to change. He did not know who his wife would become, if she got well. He knew how to play his present role. A new way of interacting would be too much.

Always in my life, I kept pushing past the stormy struggles that came from outside me, and those that lingered inside me. So occupied with struggles was I, that I did not notice just how I landed in a safe harbor. There were rare moments in the past that I felt that I had arrived in a peaceful place and then the feeling vanished.

Now I know that experiencing safety consists of what I have already, i.e., fulfilling friendships, sufficient self-trust, and meaningful service.

While remaining aware that life includes obstacles to overcome, my consistent present experience is an exciting adventure. Everyday is unique and satisfying. Like everyone, I am an evolving being. Having sailed to a port of peace, I have what was missing earlier in my life.

Unable to substitute the challenging experiences that I had for positive imaginary one, I played with the notion that I could imagine a loving childhood of my dreams. Momentarily pleasant, it did not last. The past crept upon me when I least expected it and I'd cringe. Even when I was not thinking of it, my awful past was there silently with its unresolved pain.

Rather than repress the past, now I accept everything that happened. No longer do I feel obligated to cover it up, nor do I continue to hide in the shadows of shame afraid to tell my story.

I am responsible for my interpretations and my reactions. Gradually, I noticed that there was love all around me in the form of friends, many of whom had been there for a very long time. Realizing that I cannot take that for granted, I discovered that it was love from many others that saved me from total chaos. It saved me to know that love is everywhere, even in people who almost never show it. It had always been there in some form or another.

Also, I have distinguished the choices that I do and did have. I learned to respond in healthier ways than suppressing myself and resenting my mother. Eventually I learned to hear what she said without allowing it to wound me. What she said and did was a manifestation of her disease.

Being in a family with the stigma of obvious mental illness and its effects, it was hard to get overly enamored of myself. From my background, I was taught that I had little value. From my adult experience, I learned that my childhood message could be a benefit or burden depending on what I do with it.

It is easy to fall into the emotional pit of a victim. When seeing myself as a victim, a background like mine is a burden. That load darkens the present moment, robbing me both then and now. If I am angry about not having happy messages, I live with anger. If I complain about what I did not get, I live with loss. Certainly this is a normal human response. It does not work for a joyful life. I would rather be happy now that be angry about the past.

When I realize I can choose my reactions, I am no longer automatically self-pitying or disgruntled.

As an adult, when in a position to choose the life I wanted, I re-directed my life. Aware I could not please my parents, I knew I might as well follow my own path.

Now I am glad that I dared to look back. Writing has supported me in coming to terms with the memories that I did not want to revisit. Though I preferred avoiding the past, by examining it, I have more compassion for both my past and present self.

For my childhood, I have no regrets. In fact, I can appreciate that this was my spiritual path. Though I did not inherit mental illness, I can see how I am like my mother. By ignoring and neglecting my physical and emotional needs and denying the severity of my lung problems, I have been as cruel to myself as she was to me. Yet, even that brought benefits. My health needs got so imperative that it stimulated the search for alternative solutions in health, career, and spirituality.

Also, my childhood engendered determination and perseverance since getting through the day took enormous exertion. As a result, I worked through the chaos I carried with me. Though I had cleaned up and rearranged clutter whenever my mother was hospitalized, I had no skill at real organization.

With my husband Ed's loving support, I learned to create physical order in the household instead of unconsciously falling into the family habits of disorder. Now thanks to Ed, I am highly organized. The emotional chaos within me has subsided, too.

At an early age, I had to learn to count on myself. Partly because I have trained myself to notice self-blame and not believe it, life feels full of joy. Though life is not always smooth, my reaction to unwanted events is generally easy. After growing up with so many daily upsets, I take all things calmly now.

By persevering in career and relationships, I gradually learned to see some of my worth. Still, I am in a process of realizing I deserve to be treated well. I have come a long way in not tolerating poor treatment that I used to accept without question.

Recognizing at a young age just how complicated human emotions, motivations, and desires were, I learned a lot about human nature. Throughout my careers, especially now as a relationship coach, I have used my early education of mentally ill parents to benefit others and myself.

What I learned was that love can be found in strange and wonderful places. It does not always have to be earned. I discovered love in daily interaction, in random acknowledgments, and in warm smiles. Love was there in the Lollipop Lady, in Danielle, in Sandy, in Mrs. Finley, in Pat the Pink Cat Lady, in Barb, and in Sr. Augustine. Love sustained me through my high school classmate inner circle, and scores of other high school and college friends. Without them, I do not think I could have come through my past. They were the bridge that took me to my present life of joy.

Relying on love as my foundation, I found the courage to trust others. The more I enjoy the people around me, the more affection keeps growing. Love is an abundant sacred garden that replenishes itself.

Now, I am healthier than I have ever been. I move with ease through life. Profoundly grateful, my days are full and flourishing with a loving, healthy husband; a joyful, successful daughter; abundant, fulfilling friendships and meaningful, rewarding work. Always, I am embracing Emerson's words: *Life is a festival only to the wise.*

I celebrate each day as a gift. Profoundly, I wish that for you, as well.

All your past except its beauty is gone, and nothing is left but a blessing.

~ The Course In Miracles

I have always believed, and I still believe, that whatever good or bad fortune may come our way we can always give it meaning and transform it into something of value.

-- Hermann Hesse

PART FOUR

GIFTS

MUSING OVER GIFTS

Overcoming is not the only goal or glory. Surviving is not really living. No matter what background you had, you need **to soar and to thrive.** Using your life for healthy purposes for yourself and others is the true victory. Finding the missing ingredients and creating something extraordinary is the result of taking what you have been given and spinning it into gold. Restructuring the old thinking and feeling into something valuable and authentic is a person's path to a life of renewal and creation.

One way to do that is to recognize those mountains that you have climbed and conquered. What's the story you tell about your past? Is it one where you are the hero or heroine? Or, is it one where you are the victim? How did the past shape you to be powerful? What are your strengths? How did those painful experiences create such intense pressure that a pearl grew out of the irritation under your proverbial shell? Did the pressure turn the coal of your suffering into a figurative diamond that reflected prisms from the sparkling light of your valuable qualities?

Fortunately for me, I met some healthy adults, such as an affable neighbor, an English teacher, and a college cook. Moreover, I had the love of people all around me: friends in schools, in neighborhoods, and beyond. They let me see myself in numerous roles other than daughter. School was a haven and a refuge, a place where I had a chance to succeed. There were other groups, such as Brownies and Girl Scouts outside of school that expanded my circle of love. All of that was crucial to creating a wedge, a break in the unrelenting, concrete tension of living at home. It provided an emotional cushion for me, one I truly needed in a household that was hostile and apathetic to my physical and emotional welfare.

As a child, there was little I could do, but endure. Seeing the world through the filter of pain, I experienced struggle continually until I questioned the real source of it. Shifting from the immediate pain and inquiring into it, I then had the choice of what to do about it. Difficulties could bring me down, or fortify me. Sometimes I went down. Other times, I landed on my feet. Somehow, I learned to thrive.

Without the challenges, I would never know how far I could go. I would not know what I could do. Without my struggles I would not be the person who is unafraid of whatever will come. My past prepared me to be self-reliant.

Never would I advocate looking for struggles. Life gives you enough of them. For me, having them early allowed me to have a chance to confront challenges without evaluating the enormity of them. At a young age, I was so busy surviving that I did not have time to judge how difficult it was. My life did not compare well to the other people I knew, but I pressed on, since that was all I had.

Some gifts that are available out of such a childhood are included in the following pages. While I do not claim to have mastered all these gifts, I had early opportunities in putting them into practice to some extent. That is an advantage for which I am grateful. Here are some strengths that I can identify in myself. I know that you have your strengths, as well. I invite you to claim these and more in yourself, as you see fit.

SELF-AWARENESS and UNDERSTANDING

Out of having to be aware of Mother's moods, I developed antennae for others' states of mind and feeling. Walking into a room of strangers, I can tell usually what is going on with each individual. My early home education required studying facial expression, body language, voice inflection and physical location. Now I can pick up on subtleties, even in a room of new people.

How did this happen? It was crucial for my safety to gauge the amount of danger I was in at any given moment. Studying my mother's ups and downs, I knew that both her highs and lows were potentially volatile. Besides that, her occasional calm states could change in a nanosecond.

Part of my first self-awareness was that I was bad. Most likely that is why, when I grew older, I was always trying to be good in order to compensate for the feeling that I was not.

The chapter BAD came out of a conversation with my friend, Jane Bath. We were discussing how we were as toddlers. Repeating what I heard about myself as a toddler, I automatically asserted that I had been a bad child.

I told her one story I heard often about me at age three. While I was a problem for my parents, I was made wrong for acting my age.

Immediately, Jane reminded me of the obvious, that a

toddler could not be bad. Although on an intellectual basis I knew that, I had not applied this knowledge to myself. Never in my life did I refer to any other toddler as bad. Yet, up until recently, I wrongly identified myself in a way I wouldn't apply to anyone else.

After that exchange, I realized that I still regarded myself as essentially bad, despite a life dedicated to making a positive difference. Grieving the years that I hated myself and hid the "bad" me, I vowed to accept the bad and the good. That brought the startling insight that trying to be good was a hopeless effort to atone for my past self-assessment.

From that awareness, I understood that I could never be good enough to stop the 'bad' label, unless I changed my perception. I acknowledged all my qualities, along with my past actions, beliefs, and decisions.

The same theme came up throughout my life. The story CRIME AND PUNISHMENT illustrates at first grade, I already assumed I was a bad person. Though I didn't have a clear reason for the label, I continued to identify with that self-image. Sure I was "bad," I continued to tense up through adulthood, every time I saw a police car. Certainly, if police were near me, I must have been doing something wrong.

Remembering my cranky behavior in HOW ICE CREAM CAN GO WRONG helps me have compassion for children, knowing how hard it was for me to be that young. That was not the only time I was difficult, for sure. My humanity comes through in FAMILY UN-TOGETHERNESS and SIBLING BONDING OVER A FREEZER. These memories remind me to give others a break.

My new self-awareness has not gone from "I am bad" to "I am good." That would be an impossible stretch. The important thing I learned is that no one is all saint or sinner. We all have the ability to go either way at any time and anywhere in between those opposites. If that were not the case, then doing the right thing would not be a choice. No one gets it right all the time, even those who do their best to lead exemplary lives.

The chapter I'LL GET IT RIGHT AWAY demonstrates that verbal abuse was a daily thing. It made me sensitive to others needs because I know what it feels like to be mocked for having needs and being oneself. In my twenties, someone asked me what my needs were. No one ever asked me that. Although I did not know what mine were, the question made me realize that needs are important. Being unaware of needs is hardly an advantage.

In SECRETS, I described learning that my brothers and I were not the only ones with a difficult time at home. It struck me that Colleen had it harder than we did. Despite realizing that silence about her life circumstance was not working for Colleen, I could not discuss her situation, or mine. At that time, there were no social services. Neighbors, teachers and church members looked the other way. No one knew what to do. Thankfully things have changed, so people can get professional help, go to a school guidance office, research information on the internet, and attend support groups. Now, you are rarely alone. Sharing your story helps your healing and that of others.

Opening up to another's pain, in GROWING PAINS: LESSONS IN THE SCHOOL YARD, I recognized that I had company in pain. I saw that I could communicate and get support just by joining in silence, or holding space for another. Throughout my life this realization has been immensely valuable. As a coach, I can trust myself, knowing that communication and connection take many forms.

In THE VBT (Very Bad Times) I showed that while our home was always acutely cluttered, the disarray at the very bad times was extreme. Living like that made me want to be organized. I did not have the skills to do that. It sounds like it would be a no-brainer. For me, it was a struggle.

The desire to be organized and clutter free stayed with me long enough to learn what to do. I had to unlearn the old ways that I witnessed and acquired. It helped that I married a man with strong organizational skills. By observation, I emulated his orderliness and practiced it regularly. I wanted to have a home environment that worked smoothly. Happily, with those skills developed, I keep a structured, smooth running home that family, friends, and I can enjoy.

INDEPENDENCE, FREEDOM, AND SELF-RELIANCE

Here are some examples of doing things on my own. In the chapter THE ORPHANAGE, at three years old the early seeds of independence were sown. While I was clear that I was dependent on adults, I felt it was unsafe to rely too much on anyone. Having this mind-set worked for me in some ways, though not always. I'll never know if relying on others would have worked better because that did not look like an option. The clear evidence in front of me indicated that I would have to find and follow my own path.

By the time I was nine, that imprint was reinforced by a TV movie about a boy whose parents died when he was young. He made his way alone through life. Identifying with the message that we are each on our own mission no matter the number of people around, I had a huge lump in my throat. Yet, I would not cry because I refused to expose my feelings about having to be responsible for me.

The gift of **self-reliance** comes from such a background as mine. Since there is little to no emotional support that I could count on from either parent, I knew that I was the one to solve my daily challenges.

In the chapter THE LONE WINDOW, this was one of the first signs to me that I wanted freedom. Looking beyond the confinement of a classroom that was mostly beneath the ground level, the window was the one access to the outside world that called to me. I treasured that. Confinement was anathema to me.

Independence asserted itself in HOMEMADE ICE CREAM, when I realized that I could say "no," at least when others are refusing, too.

Knowing that I had to rely on myself made me aware I needed a profession. So, I plotted to get away to a college where I could be free of parental interference. Still, I was and am grateful for the college funding.

A breakthrough in taking control of my life came in YELLOW PAGES, when I told my father that he needed to call a psychiatrist for Mother.

Not allowing Mother's behavior to run my life is exemplified in NO ESCAPE FROM MOTHER.

With dignity, I stood up to authority while having no agreement in the chapter THE PRINCIPAL.

Knowing that I was on my own, led to preparation. Babysitting and saving the money, allowed me to purchase a car.

In the DRIVING chapter, I described the freedom I obtained from that car. Besides earning money by driving friends to school, the car also provided the means to satiate my physical and emotional hunger.

All through life I took ever-bigger adjustments as I went along. For example, before flying alone to Cincinnati for college, I knew not one person, not one contact outside of the name of the inaccessible college president on the brochure.

When I took a teaching position as a reading specialist in New Jersey, I knew no one and was unfamiliar with the town and the state. Independently, I traveled around eleven countries in Europe for eight weeks before the advent of the internet. Relocating to New York City to work as a writer, I knew only the name of a friend of a friend.

Several times I decided to leave employment, without another means of security. And once, I chose to separate from my husband without any safety net.

PERSEVERANCE AND PREPARATION

As described in QUASIMODO, it took massive amounts of energy to get through the day with asthma and emphysema. Even without the breathing challenge, nothing was physically easy for me in the house of horrors with dust, dirt, and clutter.

The chaos was emotional and physical. There was little or no heat in the winter and no cool air in the summer. As a result of moving through exceptional discomfort, I don't give up easily. Self-discipline developed, though hopefully not in a controlling way.

Having a chronic illness brought frustration and shame. That, along with my home environment, was an especially difficult combination.

Having to persevere through the day with a physical struggle brought an unstoppable quality to my life. I had no choice but to keep moving forward. My lung issues have not completely healed. I've made friends with it. Well maybe not BFF, but I have an acceptance and tolerance that I didn't have in my youth. It was a bumpy ride ... actually more like open warfare with me losing BIG every time I resisted. In 1985, I had lung capacity tests showing I had 16% of my lung capacity. It is now 38%. Pulmonologists are surprised. The message I wused to get was that my lungs could not improve. No one tells me that anymore.

Technically, I could have said: "It's too hard. I can't go on." Yet, the only option outside of moving on was to stay there in my parents' home. That was a worse fate than braving the elements and swimming upstream against the current.

Experience taught me that if I had to do something I could do it, no matter what. I pushed the limits of physical strength and emotional resolve. The quiet determination that grew within supported me throughout my life.

PATIENCE, FLEXIBILITY AND RESILIENCE

Having to wait years to break out of my home, I learned to see the long view. It takes patience to find meaning while biding your time.

In MY HOMEWORK AND A BOY'S, this incident put me on notice that life was not secure. After that, I wanted to be vigilant to Mother's ups and downs, in an effort to control my surroundings. What I discovered was that though I could control nothing and I could predict nothing, I needed to stay present so I could choose quickly my next move in the moment.

In the MORNING story, inner strength was already well practiced. Mother's late night antics of waking me were just one of the plethora of ways that gave me the discipline of patience and tolerance.

Often dogs that are naturally pleasant and pliable are ones that were harassed early in life and stressed by a thoughtless child, or adult. Anyone born with an unmedicated mentally ill parent tends to experience some mistreatment. That can result in building a higher than normal tolerance for the *slings and arrows of outrageous fortune*. (Shakespeare. *Hamlet*)
The early experiences allowed me to take life in stride.

Serious challenges don't easily ruffle me. To this day, I can take shocking news with tranquility and serenity.

The chapter A LIVING PIN CUSHION illustrates that developing tolerance helped me stay calm in the midst of emotional storms.

Though I was PLEASING DAD, I was patiently building a relationship with a remote parent. There was little I would not do to make that relationship work. Without any interest in baseball, I learned the rules of the sport, learned the Phillies team members, collected and traded ball cards and played the game with the boys. To please, I drank awful tasting alcohol. I did whatever it took to connect through Dad's interests.

THE DANCE illustrates that I had pretended not to care at first. This was one example of having a healthy detachment to the dances, without being submissive to the circumstance. Taking my stand, I willingly paid the price.

In my life, there were many times when anger surfaced. I would capture it like a small, dangerous panther and shut it in its cage. The next challenge was to practice like an emotional gymnast on a balance beam, to do all I could to avoid falling into the pit of anger and resignation. Often I fell into the pit before I got on the beam and before I could find the right balance. Even at those times I managed to surrender to what was happening without the wasted angst.

In COLLEGE PLAN, I began to experience my ability to shape my life. For many years, I had been mentally preparing for this break. I took what life had given me. What I did not like, I ignored as much as possible. What I did like, I used to the maximum.

ALTRUISM AND COMPASSION

Intimately understanding what hunger and deprivation is, I don't want others to experience that. I want everyone in every country and in the world to have the opportunity to feed themselves and live happily. Going beyond wanting, I continue to make that goal a reality through The Hunger Project, an International Organization for the global end of hunger.

Over the years I observed the underlying unhappiness my mother carried. Even in the singing, dancing moments, she was clearly faking a mood she couldn't access. She forced the 'good' moods and I could hear and see the anger underneath. In a moment those expressions could morph into raw aggression. Even when they didn't turn, the acid bitterness and palpable sadness in her was present in the outward, driven attempt to hide it.

When I grew up and away from Mother, I realized she could not help herself. No one would want to be that way she seemed compelled to be.

Compassion for others with physical challenges developed early in me. I am sure it had everything to do with knowing how problematic and tough life could be.

In WHO DO YOU THINK YOU ARE!, I learned that being shamed is painful. Realizing that no one else deserves that, I vowed to never do that to another.

The chapter SOUNDS tells one of many stories of growing up with a mother expressing the odd behavior of making bizarre sounds constantly for long periods of time. It helped me to have insight into a world where strange behavior occurs in many people.

THE ESSAY is an example of how little acknowledgment occurred in our home. No one received recognition. Longing for some response, I became sensitive to how deprivation felt and observed where it was missing for others. Knowing how important acknowledgment is, I could offer it more easily to others. After awhile, a strange thing happened. Personally, I needed less affirming. In the act of giving recognition to others, I felt affirmed. What I gave, I received.

In VISITING THE HOSPITAL, the shock for me was realizing that a young, attractive woman who seemed stable could be mentally ill. It gave me more empathy and more open-mindedness. At the time, I still could not grant full compassion for my hostile mother.

For years, I struggled with a dilemma. Knowing my mother was sick, I could not rationally fault her. Yet, I did not get my needs met. I was a walking open wound. Since then, I slowly nurtured myself and accepted the authentic love of others. I understood that Mother had little or no control over her words or actions. Not loving herself, she couldn't love me.

When I first read the words of Dr. Karl Menninger: "Love cures people both the ones who give it, and the ones who receive it," I immediately realized that I had been living by that inner knowing. I have always known that giving love and receiving love are one and the same.

DISCOVERING LOVE, GRATITUDE, AND INTEGRITY

Every joy is heightened since I didn't have it when I was young. Feelings of unworthiness led to proving myself to the world. I learned to keep my word no matter what it cost me. The fear of letting others down, I figured, kept others from dismissing me, as I thought they would. Very motivated to be included, eventually I absorbed the feeling of being accepted. That was something that transformed me. I felt sheer gratitude for people's love.

Also, having to prove my value, I trained myself to live with integrity. I did what I had to do until I did my best. At first, it may have been to win friends. Later, it was purely because I wanted to.

The years of having little to eat and too few comforts to mention, made me value what I had. I can truly relish the smallest things in life because I have experienced breaking through the concrete of life and emerging into the light most of the time. The dark calls to me and finds me when I'm not vigilant.

The small amount of healthful, stimulating experiences made me seek for deeper meaning and substance in my life. It made me want to give authentic service to those who have less than I do.

The shame of having a discernible illness, a visible rash, and an obvious, dysfunctional family brought me insight into how others feel. Gradually, I began to accept the parts of me that brought such shame. Not always am I successful at loving all parts of me, but each day I am a bit closer to wholeness than ever before.

Naomi was one who gave me love when I was too young to know and appreciate it. In later years, I have wondered how much I owe Naomi for contributing to me. She seemed all that my mother wasn't. In the short meeting, I knew from Naomi's generous spirit that she must have held me and loved me when I was a baby. Most likely, she protected me at times from Mother's rage.

More appreciation is shown in the chapter WHEN THE SUN BROKE THROUGH. Seeing my serious father smile might seem a small thing, and it was huge for me. It lit me up.

In SIBLING BONDING OVER A FREEZER, hunger on a regular basis made me appreciate food when I got it. Often I had to forage for it as a child and teen.

LOVE THY NEIGHBOR tells how a neighbor's love nurtured and sustained me. Mrs. Finley empowered me with her attention and her concern for my health.

GENEROSITY is one incident of many that taught me non-attachment to physical things. While I still can get temporarily attached to things, this is an example of a big lesson. Having no control of incoming or outgoing things, I knew I could not afford to hold on to anything. If I let my feelings take over, I would lose. I was not going to get the dress back and I was not going to let that fact sacrifice my spirit. Also, it taught me that people could be enormously big-hearted. Continually now I am surprised and delighted by people's generous spirit.

Glimpsing some love in my mother, GIVING AND RECEIVING was a shocking discovery, though I forgot it often after that. Giving me candy did not fit with the angry, withholding mother I knew. It taught me that no matter how much I think I know someone, there is another side to her or him, even if I do not see it more than a few times. It helps me to remember that when I am tempted to demonize someone.

The TELEPHONE story shows that I can disappoint another, be let down myself, and continue to love and be loved.

My AFTER SCHOOL experience showed a change in my mother. In this rare occasion, her narcissism was eclipsed by her concern for me. Though it did not signal a lasting trend, it was safe to ask for help that once. It was another example of my mother's hidden side.

ENCOURAGEMENT IN A NUN'S GARB told the story of a nun who believed in me. It was like sunshine and water on a plant, bringing me to life.

In LIFE IS TENUOUS, I learned that a freak accident could take away anyone's ability to move. This sobering thought put me in touch with mortality. Witnessing Judy's struggles, I was grateful for mobility. At her funeral, I knew how fortunate I was to be alive.

RESPONSIBILITY

The incident described in MONEY, and the family culture of miserly non-spending, contributed to making me very responsible about money. It began out of fear of misplacing things and of losing money myself.

Like anything, the extreme of a good thing, like thrift, can have a dark side. Growing up, there was no real joy in giving or receiving things. There was not any freedom or generosity. It took me a long time to open up to spending even a little beyond the necessities. It took decades before I could spend money on myself.

Financially and in all areas of my life, I took responsibility for my choices and actions. I did not look to my parents for help, or look to them to blame. Obviously, I made my choices to go my way, even when it displeased my parents, my relatives, or my friends.

DETACHMENT

In the chapter THE BELOVED DOLL, I saw that having to give up attachment to things came at an early age. However, it gave me another perspective by seeing that things were only things. As a child, I felt powerless over people and things. By having to give that up, I longed for what was truly important. Getting my heart broken over a damaged doll, or broken records, or lost clothing were early lessons in finding emotional flexibility and seeking true value.

THE STATUE points to an incident when having the time to notice a wider range of people, I learned a great deal about human nature. When my mother came and gave away my prize, it was a lesson on releasing even though it was not easy. It was clear that keeping the temporary relationship with Sara was more important to me than my prize possession.

In BREAK IN, BREAKTHROUGH, the turning point allowed me to see my emotional strength. Not only did I see Mother's manipulation, I did not allow myself to get emotionally caught up in it. The hardest thing was not making myself wrong. Also, I did not let myself worry about the possibility of bad public opinion. People would have to think whatever they chose. It had little to do with me.

CAR FOLLOW UP was about releasing frustration. As long as I was dependent financially on my parents for college tuition, I knew that even my car that I worked and paid for was not considered my own. Being upset about it was fruitless when it could not change any-thing. To move on, I had to dissipate the frustration. I learned to be practical and resilient about reality.

INSIGHTS AND PERSPECTIVES

WHO DO YOU THINK YOU ARE?
The question was so prevalent that I saw it differently over a decade later. It came up front and center when I was married and living in NJ. While there are many examples, the following story is just one.

When I became a mother my parents did not come to visit me. There were not angry with me. It just was inconvenient.

Living 92 miles away, Ed and I drove to them to present my infant daughter. Setting the date weeks in advance, I called to remind them before I left. Dad answered and assured me it was fine to visit that day.

When Dad came to the door that day, I was smiling in awe of the wonder of birth. I said to Dad of my newborn: "Isn't she beautiful? Look, ten tiny toes and ten little fingers." Catching a glimpse of Dad I saw deep distain, as if I had committed the worst social sin possible. To him, I had. I assured him that I was humbled by this baby's existence as a gift from God. Since my daughter did not have my features, I told him honestly that I was not taking credit for her perfection.

My explanation did not matter. I could hear the silent, but palpable, words: "Who do you think you are!" It made me tear up thinking that his answer was always: "Nobody. And nothing."

Unbeknownst to me, Mother was in a mental hospital.

I was stunned that Dad's shame kept him from revealing it to me. I would have come at a different time. Dad did not think it was a problem that Mother could not see her first grandchild, since she was too sick to be allowed visitors at the mental hospital. When she did get out, I came back. Mother did not seem too interested, anyway.

I realized that Dad's look that said: "Who do you think you are!" was his self-assessment, not just aimed at his children and grandchild. It certainly had nothing to do with this perfect baby that I held in my arms. So it wasn't about others. My dad carried that pain. I no longer would.

The incident described in the chapter WHAT IS ACCEPTABLE? gave me the opportunity to think deeply about what society expected. At a young age, it appeared that what is expected is what affected the onlooker directly, not about what might be underneath the surface of the unacceptable behavior. If someone would lie down on the lawn, it was not acceptable. If they publicly attacked, hit, and slapped their small children after chasing them down the street, that was all right in those days. What are we accepting or not accepting in society now that is just as insane?

In the story THE CALM AND THEN THE STORM, this is one example of when I understood that some people use religion to promote self-righteousness and to curb joy. Too much religion at the wrong time can be an expression of deep guilt and self-hate.

Right up until now, my mind tells me dumb stuff everyday. I do not think that will ever stop. For instance, my mind suggests that I do not have to exercise everyday. I exercise anyway. It tells me that I should not have to do hard things now because I'm getting older, I'm truly tired, I did enough … you name it. I do what needs to be done anyway.

Now I make each day count. Not guaranteed another day, I enjoy the one I'm in. Still progressing, I continue to unearth the treasure in my past while I stay present and relish the moment.

PART FIVE

SURVEY

*We go through those circumstances
in order to evolve into people
who can hold to our loving center
no matter what the world throws us.*
~ Marianne Williamson

SURVEY RESULTS

Many people have made this kind of journey that I have made. This is my version from my experience. In describing the path out of my personal torment, I hope to spark a vision for your life beyond what you presently perceive.

These are the results of a recent survey I designed in February 2011. These statistics indicate that the emotional health of our nations children is not the healthiest it could be. Too many of us grow into adulthood with a level of unresolved issues. Obviously, I am not alone in my experience.

Eighty-four adults, each over forty years old, responded. These are the survey results with the number of respondents:

When I was a child, I was taken care of physically, mentally and emotionally by both parents.

Parental Support		Comments
Strongly Disagree	22	This question asked if people were supported mentally, physically and emotionally when they were growing up. The largest number responded by **disagreeing that they were supported fully.** That leaves a lot of room for improvement.
Disagree Somewhat	21	
Agree	9	
Agree Somewhat	18	
Strongly Agree	12	
Not Applicable	2	

I still have unresolved issues with my mother.

Parental Support		Comments
Strongly Disagree	32	**The majority appears to be experiencing resolution with their mother .** While some checked this question as not applicable, I think that this question is applicable, even if a parent is no longer living.
Disagree Somewhat	17	
Agree	13	
Agree Somewhat	10	
Strongly Agree	5	
Not Applicable	7	

I still have unresolved issues with my father.

Parental Support		Comments
Strongly Disagree	26	**Issues with fathers appear to be more unresolved than issues with mothers.**
Disagree Somewhat	19	
Agree	11	
Agree Somewhat	14	
Strongly Agree	8	
Not Applicable	6	

My unresolved issues with one, or both, my parents still affects me negatively.

Parental Support		Comments
Strongly Disagree	29	**Happily, the majority does not identify negative effects on them from their childhood.** A lot may depend on how a person views their past at any given time. Those that said: "Disagree Somewhat" still could agree on various areas of their upbringing.
Disagree Somewhat	13	
Agree	11	
Agree Somewhat	12	
Strongly Agree	11	
Not Applicable	8	

I grew up believing that life was difficult.

Parental Support		Comments
Strongly Disagree	12	**The overwhelming majority of the respondents agreed that in childhood they believed that life was hard.**
Disagree Somewhat	15	
Agree	19	
Agree Somewhat	10	
Strongly Agree	25	
Not Applicable	3	

I know of a relative other than my parents that was mentally unstable.

Parental Support		Comments
Strongly Disagree	13	**Having an unstable relative seems to be very common.**
Disagree Somewhat	7	
Agree	18	
Agree Somewhat	6	
Strongly Agree	28	
Not Applicable	12	

Since I received most of my nurturing from my family, I did not need to look outside my family.

Parental Support		Comments
Strongly Disagree	29	This question asked if people felt they received so much nurturing that they did not need to go outside their family to find it. **A large number agreed that they needed to go outside for nurturing.**
Disagree Somewhat	21	
Agree	12	
Agree Somewhat	12	
Strongly Agree	8	
Not Applicable	2	

I was as prepared for adulthood as possible due to my parents positive influence.

Parental Support		Comments
Strongly Disagree	24	This question asked if respondents were prepared for adulthood. **Most people felt unprepared for adulthood.** Could parents do more in this area, or is it a rite of passage for children to feel unprepared?
Disagree Somewhat	26	
Agree	11	
Agree Somewhat	12	
Strongly Agree	8	
Not Applicable	3	

Valued and respected, I have a sense of importance and self-esteem that grew from interactions with my parents.

Parental Support		Comments
Strongly Disagree	26	**The majority disagreed that they were valued as a child.** I wonder what results would be shown if this question about being valued would be asked of young children today.
Disagree Somewhat	20	
Agree	17	
Agree Somewhat	12	
Strongly Agree	3	
Not Applicable	3	

I had at least one personal experience of being in danger at the hands of one or both of my parents.

Parental Support		Comments
Strongly Disagree	40	**The majority did not feel that they were in danger from one or both parents.** Hooray for that.
Disagree Somewhat	9	
Agree	5	
Agree Somewhat	8	Yet, a significant number did feel in some danger.
Strongly Agree	19	
Not Applicable	6	

Other books by the author include:

Overcomers, Inc **includes Marifran Korb's story***:***
The Weed that Grew Out of the Sidewalk
You can view and purchase a copy here:
http://soulfulsolutions.com/services/ by clicking
"Buy Book" on this page.

Travel Tips For Ireland: What The Experts Forgot
to Tell You. **A Kindle book.** http://tiny.cc/nw7jjw

Breaking Through Concrete: The Gifts of Having
Mentally Ill Parents **can be found on Kindle.**

To contact the author, write
Marifran@MentallyIllParents.com

Websites and Blogs:

www.SoulfulSolutions.com
http://MentallyIllParents.com
http://MarifranKorb.com

I am not what happened to me.
I am what I choose to become.
~ Carl Jung

www.ingramcontent.com/pod-product-compliance
Lightning Source LLC
Chambersburg PA
CBHW051944090426
42741CB00008B/1270